WITNESSING GWANGJU

A MEMOIR

This book is dedicated to the people of Gwangju,
of Jeonnam Province, and all of Korea.

Witnessing Gwangju

All royalties from the sale of the book will go to support the important prevention of blindness work carried out by the Kilimanjaro Centre for Community Ophthalmology (www.kcco.net).

Published by Hollym International Corp., Carlsbad, CA, USA
Phone 760 814 9880
www.hollym.com   **e-Mail** contact@hollym.com

 Hollym

Published simultaneously in Korea
by Hollym Corp., Publishers, Seoul, Korea
Phone +82 2 734 5087   **Fax** +82 2 730 5149
www.hollym.co.kr   **e-Mail** hollym@hollym.co.kr

ISBN: 978-1-56591-495-7
Library of Congress Control Number: 2020932609

Printed in Korea

The contents of this book represent the views and opinions of the individual author and do not necessarily represent the opinions of Hollym.

WITNESSING GWANGJU

A MEMOIR

Paul Courtright

 Hollym

Carlsbad, CA and Seoul

Author's note

—

The events described in this book occurred in 1980, almost forty years ago. Recounting them was possible because of detailed notes and letters I wrote during and just after the thirteen days described in this memoir. Reading through my notes always triggers a flood of memories, comprised of conversations, emotions, and images. Memories can be faulty and I acknowledge that I'm no different from the rest of humanity—there may be some unintended errors in my retelling. I've done the best I could to be objective, but my objectivity was challenged by the events I witnessed. Conversations are difficult to recreate, particularly as a sixty-four-year-old retelling the words of a twenty-five-year-old. Consequently, some colleagues and friends may say "I don't remember saying that." Fair enough.

After I finished a few drafts of the memoir I decided that I needed to revisit sites in Gwangju, Nampyeong, and Hohyewon to link the images in my memory with the places. It was tough. Korea has undergone massive change in the last forty years. Gwangju has expanded beyond belief. Nampyeong is no longer a "wide spot in the road." Hohyewon has virtually ceased to exist; it's mostly abandoned, having been swallowed up, bit by bit, by expanding factories. Nevertheless, my trip in May 2019 helped me to recapture some of the sights, sounds, and smells. In Nampyeong a friend and I got a taxi to take us to Hohyewon. The taxi driver, about my age, was surprised that I knew of Hohyewon, given its obscurity and rapid abandonment. We chatted and I learned that his brother was killed during 5.18 (as the Gwangju Uprising is now called). He was on the road between Gwangju and Nampyeong when the military opened fire on his vehicle. I was on that road.

When I arrived in Seoul in May 2019, I was shocked to learn that the multitude of stories from 5.18 has not been fully captured and that there are people in Korea today questioning whether it actually happened. It happened. Some were saying that it was a communist insurrection, orchestrated or supported by North Korea. No, it was not. Some called it a riot by unruly students. No, it was not. At the request of friends and colleagues, I ended up doing interviews for newspapers, TV, and blogs. I felt that I couldn't say "no."

Telling my story of 5.18 was important for me—partly to bring some closure to a traumatic period in my life. I hope that, as a foreigner who lived in the area at the time, my story will also help the healing still needed in Gwangju and the surrounding towns and villages. Finally, I hope that Westerners will better appreciate the importance of this event in the history of Korea and Korean-American relations. Korea's history is intertwined with America's and the more we learn from both, the better off we all will be in making informed decisions in the future.

Paul Courtright
July 8 2019

Contents

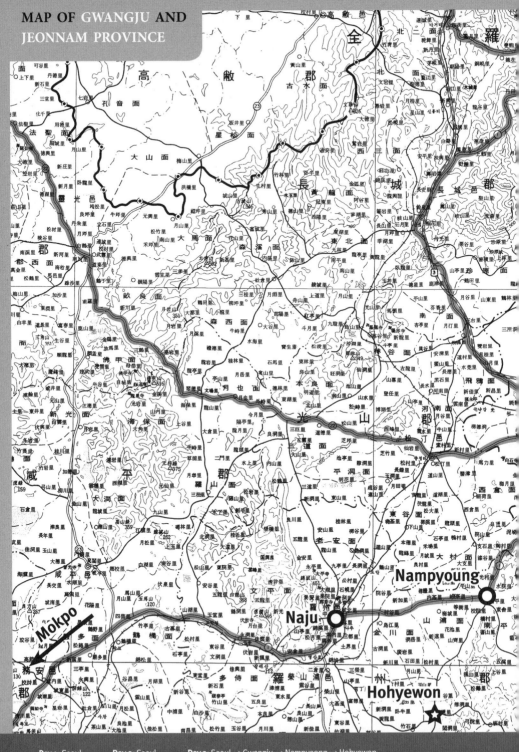

MAP OF GWANGJU AND JEONNAM PROVINCE

Mokpo

Nampyoung

Naju

Hohyewon

Map of South Korea

Day 4: Hohyewon   **Day 5:** Between Hohyewon and Gwangju   **Day 6:** Gwangju → Suncheon → Gwangju

Day 9: Hohyewon → Naju → Nampyeong → Gwangju   **Day 10:** Gwangju   **Day 11:** Gwangju

Prologue

—

The morning May sun warmed me as I walked the couple of kilometers to the Gwangju post office. I'd been back in Korea a little over a month and I carried a letter to post home to my parents in Boise, Idaho. My father's esophageal cancer diagnosis in March and the doctor's prognosis of his future—six months to five years—left me uncertain and fearful. Was it the right decision to return to Korea?

But my uncertainty and fear were nothing compared to what I saw that morning on the faces of Koreans trying to go about their lives. They were scared, but they were also angry—and for good reason. There was a scattering of charred taxis and buses askew in the road, itself littered with stones and sidewalk tiles. I walked quickly with my head up—to ensure that the unmistakable features of a "round eye" were visible to the soldiers who clustered on street corners. The previous night they were on the prowl to arrest young people. While young, I was not their target—I was an American. In my mind, however, the soldiers had become the enemy.

Safe in the cool confines of the post office, I bought the stamps, affixed them to the letter, and dropped it in the post box. The serenity of the place soothed my frayed nerves.

A tear gas canister shattered a window about thirty meters from the post box and the serenity I enjoyed evaporated. The clerks, mostly young women in their early twenties, working before getting married, bolted—most out the front door. I had become familiar with tear gas in the last few days and quickly joined them to escape out the front.

At the top of the half-dozen steps of the old redbrick post office, I paused. The street below started to fill up with people—angry people. They jeered at the soldiers stationed at the end of the block. The equivalent of "shame on you" echoed along the street of two- and three-story buildings.

Below me on the street, a civilian policeman was surrounded by people from all walks of life, firing questions at him from all directions. Their anger was directed outward, not at him. They were passionate but respectful. "Why are the soldiers—our brothers—treating us this way? Why did they kill our sons and daughters?" The policeman bowed low in respect as he responded to an elderly man. He said he was as confused as they were. He didn't know why the soldiers had attacked the people of his, of their, town. His message to anyone within hearing distance was clear—keep young people inside, protected.

I looked across the narrow street at the print or stationery shops, shops that offered to wrap items to ship, or *gage* (small shops) that sold snacks, beer, soda, and cigarettes. Small teahouses filled many of the upper floors. They were all still open, keen to provide the services desired by the residents of Gwangju. The street was tense before I walked into the post office, but now it was at a breaking point. It was time to get out of here and back to my home, in the small village of Hohyewon, not too far from Gwangju.

As I went down the steps and strode into the street, an elderly Korean *halmeoni*—a grandmother—dressed in a traditional *hanbok* of pink and green grabbed my arm, startling me. There was still a little tear gas in the air that swirled around us, but it was not debilitating. I was ready to help the *halmeoni* into a nearby *gage*, but that wasn't what she had in mind. The *halmeoni's* grip tightened on my arm and she turned to face me.

"We have no voice. You have to be our voice. You have to tell people outside our country what they're doing to us." She glanced around the street, then returned her fearless gaze to me. I was rooted to the spot. I was to be the "witness" and she had given me a clear task.

I failed the *halmeoni*. I was given a responsibility that now, forty years later, I can finally face. I hope I'm not too late.

What does it mean to be a witness? The word carries a sense of responsibility, and part of that is to give an honest voice about an event. The trouble is, the event that unfolded in front of me had no defined beginning or end. It took place over a large expanse of territory and I could not cover it all. Although just starting, it would unfold over many days and involve many people. How can I, a witness, capture it all? I cannot. In the end, all I can do is tell what I saw, what I heard, and how I felt. What I witnessed forty years ago is as real to me today as it was then.

Day 1

Wednesday, May 14:

Demonstration curiosity for the uninitiated

—

In mid-May 1980, I was a second-year Peace Corps Volunteer in South Korea. I worked in a tiny leprosy resettlement village called Hohyewon in Jeonnam Province, about thirty minutes from the city of Gwangju. I'd moved to Hohyewon from the small town of Naju, a few months before, to provide care for skin ulcers, manage drug treatments and the immunologic reactions that some patients faced, and provide basic eye care. The health center staff in Naju, where I was based the first half-year of my service, weren't happy that I moved to the village—they seemed to like having a "round eye" around, likely because I was an oddity. On top of that, they believed I was crazy to trade life in the small town for life in the leprosy village. Life in Hohyewon was more challenging than in Naju, but I'd settled into a manageable routine and my language skills had moved beyond the rudimentary. That routine was about to be upended.

The Peace Corps health education road show in tiny rural villages near the demilitarized zone in Gangwon Province had just ended. The glow of success and probably a bit too much *soju* (Korean distilled liquor) made the packed bus ride south to Seoul fairly painless. I was the only team member who worked in the deep south of South Korea and as I bounced along the mountainous back roads to get to Seoul, I imagined that my compatriots were already back at their respective health centers enjoying a well-deserved lie-in.

The bus deposited me at the well-organized but perpetually crowded Seoul bus terminal. The air buzzed with the concerned voices of students, parents, and businessmen. Seoul university students had moved their "demos," as the demonstrations were called, off-campus. As I made my way through the crowd, I heard hushed questions and statements: "How'll the military and police respond?" "Why are students doing this? It'll only cause trouble." "They should go back to their studies." "They shouldn't move their demo off-campus."

Seven months earlier, the long-serving president or military dictator (the term I used depended upon whom I was talking to), Park Chung-hee, had been assassinated and his prime minister, Choi Kyu-ha, took over. Choi decided that Korea was ready for democracy, released many political leaders, and scheduled elections—these were heady times. Less than two months later General Chun Doo-hwan mounted a military coup—Chun apparently did not share the view that Korea was ready for democracy. Everything was uncertain: Would elections be held? Would the Koreans' hard-won economic progress falter? Would people placidly accept more years of dictatorship?

I switched from the old rural bus for a newer, although still belching, city bus and I was now standing in the middle of the aisle, gripping a leather strap to avoid being thrown onto my fellow passengers. The bus wound through some grimy parts of Seoul, then into some rather posh parts before it dropped into the downtown area. Tomorrow was my annual medical checkup—an event I had delayed multiple times and could delay no longer. After almost two weeks away at the health road show, I was ready to get home to Hohyewon. I was somewhat bummed that I had to spend two nights in Seoul.

I had never liked Seoul. It was crowded and polluted. Seoul today was no different. The sky was dull. As an Idaho boy, I really didn't like many big cities. I stepped off the bus a few blocks from the center of town and saw that the action on the streets ahead was anything but dull. Near the Peace Corps office, I joined a small crowd of spectators. The normally vehicle-choked six-lane road was now choked with university students. The students sat in the middle of the street and, on cue, sang a patriotic ballad. I wondered, how the heck did they all agree on what to sing? The answer was up the street—there were a half-dozen student leaders with megaphones and whistles. The students were well-organized. Roles were clear. Actions were clear. Had they thought through the possible consequences of those actions?

Since arriving in Korea I'd never felt any sense of danger or risk—there was virtually no violent crime in the country. The scene in front of me elicited no sense of concern for my safety—if anything, the scene made me feel euphoric. Here were people standing up for what they felt was right and just, challenging a brutish military dictatorship.

The ugly but functional office blocks and quickly rising modern buildings disgorged their workers for the day and the number of spectators swelled. The students continued their polite and respectful demonstration. Marching was followed by sitting. Sitting led to singing. Singing was followed by standing, marching, and chanting. The level of organization and the fervor of the students was mesmerizing. My Korean co-spectators, however, seemed to be less impressed—this was a disruption in the social fabric of society. "Students need to study. People need to work. Our country needs progress. We don't have time for this."

I weaved around the growing knot of spectators to get a good view. I'd never seen such a large well-organized demonstration. Vietnam War protests were chaotic in comparison. This was the opposite. This was disciplined and respectful. Listening to the national anthem and other patriotic songs drift through the air was both uplifting and spellbinding. What a great sense of national pride! It amazed me that all Koreans could sing, or at least they lacked the self-consciousness about singing so common in American society.

Peering past the student leaders down to the end of the next block I saw a very different scene—a scene that could've been out of *Star Wars*. Police that looked like storm troopers had blocked the students from moving—and they were just as organized and disciplined as the students. The sight of menacing black-armored carriers backing up the police sent a shiver through me. I was intimidated. Still, the students, men and women alike, remained calm. My co-spectators and I peered at both groups with fascination. My natural inclination was to side with the students.

At 176 centimeters I'm not particularly tall, but I stood a few centimeters higher than the *ajumeoni* (aunts or married women) and stooped-over *halmeoni*, so I could easily see what was going on. Of course, as a foreigner, I stood out. Although it had taken some time, I'd learned to accept being an oddity. Most days I was the only foreigner for kilometers around and being stared at, particularly by children, had ceased to annoy me. I still didn't like it when a *halmeoni* came up to me to try to pluck any errant chest hair protruding from my shirtfront. The *halmeoni* around me today were watching a more interesting show on the street.

The ginkgo saplings planted about ten years ago struggled to claim their space on the bricked sidewalk. They'd leafed out earlier in the spring and softened the transition between the brick buildings and the street. I suspected that everyone was glad that the trees were not large enough to block the view.

The usual smell of diesel exhaust from the multitude of city buses was now absent. The smells of the human city, from small food stalls to the lingering charcoal residue of heating bricks, reclaimed their space. This was a combination of smells I'd learned to love in Korea.

Back up the street, police photographers took pictures of the student leaders and those in the front rows of the protest. I imagined police knocking on their parents' doors. Police accounts would lead to these parents' embarrassment and promises to assist their misguided children to put their energies to study instead of protest. Study was the way to get ahead—all must sacrifice to ensure a bright future for every Korean. I also imagined that the parents might listen politely to the police but, deep down, feel proud of their children. The tradition of student protest to nudge Korea to a more equitable economic system, to start the country down a road to democracy, or to vent frustration with the rigid society they lived in was hundreds of years old, starting from the introduction of Confucianism in the country. Students led the protests against the thirty-five years of Japanese occupation from 1910 to 1945 and helped to overthrow a corrupt president, Rhee Seung-man, in 1960. Education was respected. Still, it was tough being young in a society that venerated age. I sighed—the pressure on parents to sacrifice for their children to get a good education seemed overwhelming sometimes.

We made a curious line of spectators—businessmen in their still-pressed suits, *halmeoni* in their *hanbok*, female shopkeepers in their shapeless pants, and I. Not everyone wanted to watch. Some people sought the nearest subway station to get home quickly. They dashed across the street in the shrinking space between the students and the police.

Whether milling around under the gingko or making a dash across the street, everyone glanced back and forth between the police and the students—two seemingly immovable groups. There was little talking in the crowd but a lot of curiosity. "It's fine to demo on campus, but why are they doing it here in the middle of Seoul?" the *ajumeoni* selling newspapers and cigarettes said behind me. "What do they hope to achieve?"

Standing nearby, a middle-aged businessman, still neatly dressed even after a long day in the office, added ominously, "Chun Doo-hwan isn't going to step down."

It was hard for me to keep quiet. As Peace Corps Volunteers we were prohibited from engaging in any political discussion with Koreans, not to mention taking any action related to the political situation. I kept my mouth shut and listened. Standing on the sidewalk, I rummaged in my day pack for my Korean-English dictionary. The dog-eared, onionskin-paged book was never out of reach and I flipped through to look up a few new words. As I stuffed the book away a shrill whistle split the air. We all jumped.

The front row of police raced forward while the back row lobbed tear gas canisters into the air. The choreographed and well-ordered demo turned chaotic as students and spectators scattered. The police, with the tear gas canisters, were now the sole choreographed team. Along with other spectators and some students, I slipped down a small side street to escape from the acrid smoke.

I decided I'd seen enough. It was time to get to a small *yeogwan* for the night. I reached the *yeogwan's* front gate and the *ajumeoni* who ran the inn answered the bell. She was not happy. "What do those students think? They should be studying, not having a demo." She then caught a whiff of the tear gas on my clothes. "Eee… what a smell!" she said, frowning with disgust.

"It's okay, I'll get my clothes cleaned when I get home," I said, trying to placate her. I'd been away from home for a long time and all of my clothes needed to be washed.

She glanced outside one last time, then locked the outside gate behind me with a mutter. "Did you eat?"

"Yes," I lied. She asked a second time and I lied a second time. I still had some crackers in my pack that would suffice for tonight. The interaction between host and guest was always a bit challenging—people were incredibly generous. The question "have you eaten?" was a common greeting. I quickly learned to say "no" not just once but often twice or three times. If I was going to accept the offer, I waited until the third time it was given. It was both fun and frustrating to figure out the day-to-day interactions needed to navigate Korean society.

With the cheap metal key the *ajumeoni* handed over, I headed off to my two-by-two-meter room—just large enough to roll out the bedding that sat against one wall. Sleeping on a mat on the floor had been an easy transition in Korea, but Korean pillows—hard, unforgiving rice-stuffed blocks—were still a challenge. I reminded myself that I could have ended up with a block of wood, which I found sometimes—always to my dismay. I took some of my smelly clothes, wrapped them in a shirt, and used that as a pillow. I munched on the crackers, careful to hide the evidence from my *ajumeoni*. I wondered if the demos had ended.

Day 2

Thursday, May 15:

Demos are neither won nor lost

—

The morning was quiet, except for the normal hum of a rapidly expanding city of just under seven million people. The air was still and pleasantly cool. The view from the front gate of the *yeogwan* suggested that the demo yesterday might have been an illusion. No tear gas canisters littered the street; nothing was out of place. Had the demo been scrubbed from history? Buses and cars filled the main roads as usual. A midnight curfew, in place since the Korean War, got most everyone off the streets by ten in the evening. The curfew provided the opportunity for cleanup to be done.

At a nearby *gage*, I sat down and the *ajumeoni* brought me a bowl of steaming ramen and kimchi (pickled vegetables) for breakfast. "We heard that the students will be doing a demo again today," she said. "They say they'll not start until the afternoon."

"Will they start before you close?" I asked as a few noodles slipped through my chopsticks.

She sighed. "Of course. We stay open until nine. At that time we usually only sell cigarettes, *soju*, and beer."

On my Peace Corps allowance, most restaurants were out of reach. Cheap ramen and kimchi were what I often ate in Seoul. Economic turmoil had preceded the coup of December and the living allowance from the Peace Corps didn't keep up with rising prices. I handed the bowl and metal chopsticks to the *ajumeoni*. "How much do I owe you?"

"Two hundred won," she said as I dug into my pocket for coins. I handed them over and walked down the street to the bus stop. Buses came and went every few minutes and the wait was short. Bus #52 pulled up and I boarded, walking unsteadily to the middle section of the bus as the driver pulled away from the curb. Seated there was a man in conversation with a younger man, who was standing and swaying to the rhythm of the bus. I hooked one leg around a pole to avoid crashing into them and fished for my dictionary. I found the word the older man had used—it meant "patriotic." I then felt like an idiot. The Korean word was made from two characters, "love" and "country," both of which I knew very well. The man had no gray hair, but the lines on his face suggested that he was elderly. His clothes drew my attention. He was dressed in a traditional gray, immaculately pressed *hanbok*. Few men wore traditional garb in Seoul. He spoke to the young man, who I presumed was a university student. The young man had his head bowed in respect to his elder.

"Is it true that you students have demanded that martial law end today at noon?" the man asked, tilting his head upward.

"Yes," said the student respectfully, without looking up.

To me, the "yes," although quietly spoken, indicated there was likely more trouble ahead.

The old man continued to regard the young man—there was no malice or even disapproval in the look. Had the old man been part of demos when he was young?

At the next stop the young man got off, but the people in the center of the bus remained quiet—was everyone as caught up in their own thoughts about the day ahead as I was?

I walked out of the hospital a few hours later. My blood had been drawn, I'd peed into a cup, and I'd answered a bunch of questions about my health. Since arriving in Korea early last year I'd dropped about four kilograms in weight. I struggled with rice and kimchi and dried seaweed for breakfast, lunch, and dinner during my first three months in Naju. The *halmeoni* I lived with must have noticed my weight loss because she started to include a fried egg on my rice in the morning and tiny salted fish and pieces of chicken or pork from time to time. These were welcome additions, although to her and all Koreans, "food" was defined as rice and different kinds of kimchi.

Moving from Naju to Hohyewon had forced me to figure out how to cook with limited options. My diet was still mostly vegetarian, with lots of cooked rice provided by my neighbors. I didn't correct their impression that I was hopeless at cooking rice properly. Hohyewon was in the business of egg production, and eggs became a major component of my diet. There was a downside to the business, though—the village smelled like chicken shit pretty much all the time. A month earlier a grateful patient gave me a massive bag of sweet potatoes, a substantial increase in my future vitamin A intake. I'd recently found a small store in Gwangju that stocked canned tuna. There were many foods that I missed—cheese, cereals, berries, and canned tuna being just a few—but my life was little different from that of my Peace Corps friends, so I saw no point in complaining.

There were about a hundred leprosy resettlement villages in Korea, ranging in population from less than twenty-five to about four hundred. Hohyewon was one of the largest. The government had established them about fifteen years earlier to get people who were still economically productive to work. Leprosy was a stigmatizing disease and many leprosy patients, particularly those with deformities, had been homeless—unable to go back to their home villages and not accepted in Korean society. The resettlement villages that the government designated did not occupy choice farmland, and many villages were distant from main populated areas. People with leprosy lose sensation in their hands and feet, and growing rice was discouraged due to the risk of damage to these extremities. Egg production was considered a safe alternative to farming and was commonplace. In fact, by the time I arrived in Hohyewon, eggs had become a booming business. I was impressed, even if I was tired of the smell of chicken shit.

Bus #52 pulled up near the hospital and I jumped on, happy to have the annual medical checkup over. This bus was not as crowded as the one in the morning, so I got to sit. The bus, jostling as always over the metal plates that would, next year, be part of a new line on the subway system, headed in the direction of the Peace Corps office, where I was going. The rhythms nudged me to plan an early morning departure to Gwangju, to pick up some tuna and other food, then to get the bus to Nampyeong, where I'd collect my bicycle and finally, pedal the four kilometers to the three-by-three-meter room that was my "home" in Hohyewon. It was a full-day trip from Seoul to home, demanding an early morning bus out of town.

The screeching of brakes snatched me from my planning.

"Everyone out. The road's blocked!" yelled the bus driver. I peered out the front of the bus. Metal police barricades stretched across the road in front of us. It was only three in the afternoon, yet people streamed out of office blocks. Doors were closed and locked up and workers were heading home early. Everyone filed, quite orderly and without panic, down the sidewalks to get to subway stations or more distant bus stops. The police presence was formidable but, without anyone to challenge them, it felt safe.

I clambered off the bus and walked toward the Peace Corps office, which occupied part of the eighth floor of a nondescript building in the middle of town. It was a good source of information as well as the latest rumors. Periodic visits were necessary to replenish my paperback book supplies—a staple for the times spent alone.

At the office, Karin, another PCV, lounged at an open window. "Wow, have you seen the lineup of police today?"

"Yeah, they've blocked off every road from here to the train station. People are leaving work early. I hear they're expecting more demos today," I responded while rifling through the small library and picking out a few paperbacks. I thought about the conversation from the morning bus ride—would the demos be bigger than yesterday? I stuffed the books into my pack and joined Karin at the window. Down in the streets, we could see that the police presence was much larger than yesterday, which answered my question about the expected size of the demos.

Within a few minutes, at the cross-street below, students emerged from the subway stations and started to gather on the streets. The numbers swelled as we watched, moving from the hundreds to the thousands in the span of fifteen minutes. Peace Corps staff clustered around every open window.

Below us, the chanting began. "Down with Chun Doo-hwan! End martial law!"

"Yeah, bloody likely," said someone in the room.

I had observed few spectators on the walk over; there seemed to be little interest in watching today. Instead of waiting to see what might happen, people scurried to get out of the way, maybe to get home, or simply to find a place that wouldn't put them in the path of tear gas. Students continued to mass from all directions. Directly below, a group coalesced and began to march. I could see similar groups forming in the distance too. Off to the side, the police organized, forming into intimidating lines. A shrill whistle sounded, followed by an arc of flying tear gas canisters.

"Quick, close the windows!" shouted one of the Peace Corps staff.

Within a minute the staff closed all of the windows, but it was too late. Tear gas had seeped in.

"Okay, everyone, let's go home," said one staff member as he grabbed his briefcase.

Karin leaned back from the now-closed window. "I sure don't want to get trapped here for the night."

Everyone hurried, with bags and purses swinging, toward the elevator or the stairs. I decided on the stairs. I heard the office doors lock as I started down and within five minutes, everyone was on the sidewalk in front of the building. The street-level view, chaotic and noisy, was quite different from the view eight stories up—upstairs it appeared as if we were watching a relatively quiet choreographed dance. In the time it took us to reach the pavement, it appeared that the choreographers had given up. The police continued to unleash tear gas, and the students retaliated by ripping up sidewalk bricks and hurling them at the police lines.

We ran—all in different directions. My *yeogwan* was on the back side of City Hall and I ran that way, alone and nervous. What the hell was I doing here?

I turned the corner, choking on tear gas, and stumbled across a road littered with bricks, sidewalk tiles, and empty tear gas canisters. I glanced up in time to see one of the *"Star Wars"* police vans burning furiously. *Oh shit.* My heart pounded from the combination of exertion and fear.

I stopped. I needed to think this through more clearly. This was much more than a few chants, a few marching students, and a few tear gas canisters. I realized that to reach the *yeogwan* would require skirting the burning police van and using one of the underground passageways to cross the road.

I raced down the wide stairs, figuring there would be no bricks and tear gas canisters to stumble over. What a mistake! I didn't know that tear gas sinks. A thick clinging fog of the noxious stuff had me and a few other innocents crying, coughing, and gasping as we ran to get to the other side as fast as possible. I didn't trample anyone or get trampled, but there were some close calls. I emerged on the other side and struggled up the stairs. Bent over and miserable, I regretted the fact that I wore contact lenses.

The sidewalk here, just like the one on the other side of the road, was littered with rock and dislodged tile. To the south of me, there were students in several disorganized groups looking like they weren't quite sure what to do next. I heard an occasional chant and saw many raised fists but little direction. To the north of me, much closer than I liked, there was a phalanx of police with their shields and helmets at the ready. I needed to get my bearings. A whistle blared again and they moved forward. I was in the middle.

Tears streamed down my face and, unconsciously, I held my breath as I sought the safety of one of the small twisting lanes nearby. I needed to get far away from this escalating clash as quickly as possible.

Many twists and turns, dead ends, and wrong ways later, I found my *yeogwan*. The *ajumeoni* opened the gate and crinkled her nose again at the smell of my clothes. "These demos are hurting my business!" was all she had to say.

I ducked inside and handed over the cash for the night, relieved to be in a safe place. In my room, I rolled out the sleeping pad. It was still early, but I needed to lie down. Lying still and staring at the light bulb dangling from the wax-papered ceiling slowed my heart rate and allowed me to gather my thoughts.

By eight it was quiet and I stuck my head out the front gate. It seemed that many of the streets had been cleared by the riot police. I could see some *gage* and restaurants open—and I was hungry. With a shrug, the *ajumeoni* opened the gate to let me out and said the very same thing she said every night. "The gate is locked at ten. Be back by then."

I walked to the same *gage* where I'd had breakfast, where I found the *gage ajumeoni* tending her little shop. She had the TV on. I sat at a small table in front of the TV and watched footage of the burning police van. The broadcaster showed a picture of a young police officer and said, "Policeman Kang Yoon-suk died earlier today."

Oh my God.

I glanced over at the *ajumeoni* and wanted to say how sorry I was, but the combination of the sad look on her face and my struggle to find the right words to say convinced me to stay quiet. This was the first death I'd heard of during a demo, and her somber mood also suggested that this was an unusual event for Korea.

She had cooked rice earlier in the day, expecting to serve it late in the afternoon. It appeared that business had been lousy. Upset as I was at the TV announcement, I was hungry. I was buoyed to have some rice, steaming in a copper rice bowl with lid. She also put out cucumber kimchi, my favorite, and a fried egg, which I put on top of my rice. I was not slowed by the set of chopsticks she gave me. I had learned how to manipulate the unique short metal chopsticks Koreans use, and my exuberance for the food made her smile.

With a cold beer, which I probably couldn't afford, this was the best meal I'd had in a long time. I was ready to go back to my village.

Day 3

Friday, May 16:

Good to be heading home

—

I woke to another overcast, pollution-choked morning in Seoul—the dust sweeping down from Mongolia continued to give an unpleasant tinge to the morning sky. Keen to get home before dark, I was up early and off to the bus station for the five-hour bus ride to Gwangju. The bus station was not packed and, Gwangju being a major terminus for southwest Korea, there were frequent departures. I bought my ticket, boarded the bus, and settled into a window seat toward the back. Within thirty minutes we had left the big-city grime of Seoul and entered the riot of green that May in Korea puts on full display. It was a far cry from yesterday's demo.

Along a smooth multilane highway, every area that was not built up was covered by rice paddies or newly planted pines. In many places the pines were in neat rows, no matter how steep the slope. Their top branches were regular, and their height never exceeded twenty meters. My love of ponderosa pines in Idaho was being equaled by my growing love of the beauty of the Korean pines. Each pine had its own unique trunk, twisting and curving gracefully before gently leading the eye to focus on the needle bunches at the tips. The Korean pines didn't have the dark red furrowed trunks of mature ponderosa pines, but their sinuous lines were mesmerizing. Watching the scenery zip by, I wondered why I hadn't tried to learn the names of all of these trees like I had with Idaho evergreens. Time to change that.

The bus continued south and the small man-made ridges sectioning off the individual rice paddies beckoned me: *come walk along me and explore.* I never tired of exploring—and there were treasures everywhere in Korea. Neatly manicured burial mounds, tiny Buddhist shrines, large Buddhist temples, and wonderfully constructed old homes, some still with thatched roofs. All seemed to call me.

Buddhist temples were particularly good at burrowing their way into my heart and mind. They were mostly perched on the mountainsides rather than down in the valleys. Their isolated placement gave them an air of serenity, matched by the tranquil sounds and movements inside. Each temple was protected by a set of temple guards—gaudily painted figures staring fiercely down upon all who entered. The temples themselves had different functions and their designs varied to make each interesting. The gracefulness of the rooflines always drew my attention. Roof tiles, made to resemble fearsome animals, lined the corners. Temples were places to go for rest and for pondering the past, present, and future. As a Peace Corps volunteer living by myself in a village, I did a lot of pondering. I was constantly on the search for isolated, little-known temples.

My relationship with Koreans and their society was still evolving. Some aspects of the culture drove me nuts, while other aspects stimulated huge respect and admiration. It was their country, not mine. I was still learning how to be a guest, but trying not to act like a foreigner. The "we" mentality of Korean society contrasted mightily with American individualism. Koreans always said "we think" or "our country" rather than "I think" or "my country." All Koreans, from the starchily dressed schoolkids to the bent-over *halmeoni*, believed they were on a pathway to economic development—and knew that it required everyone to work as one. As I watched the students in Seoul, I wondered if some Koreans thought they were on a pathway to political development too.

Learning about the Korean culture helped me learn more about my American culture. What were aspects of it that drove me nuts? What did I respect? Would I adopt any characteristics of Korean life and culture and make them part of my own? I had little doubt that I would continue the practice of taking off my shoes before entering a house. What else would I adopt?

My need to think about the work in Hohyewon crowded out these thoughts. There would be time later to explore rice paddies and temples. The coming week was going to be busy. I had to visit a number of leprosy patients with skin ulcers, mostly on their feet and hands. They needed follow-up to be sure that they kept their wounds clean and protected. Before I left on this trip, one of my patients was having a leprosy-related immunologic reaction. He was in pain and I was worried about him. He was supposed to go to the provincial leprosy clinic for more specialized care, but I had no idea if he'd gone or not. He was not in good shape.

Most of my patients, particularly those with visible deformities, were reluctant to travel outside of our little village. Leprosy carried a considerable stigma in Korean society, and leprosy patients did their best to shield themselves and their families from the indignities of being stared at and shunned. I planned to take two men and a woman who needed eyelid surgery to a hospital in Suncheon on Monday. I hoped that my presence on the various buses needed to get there would deflect attention to me instead of them.

Over the past few months, it had dawned on me that the amount of work to be done in Hohyewon was more than I'd first imagined. In the painstaking and tedious task of copying by hand all of the patient records so I had a copy for my use, I'd come to realize that Hohyewon residents hadn't received consistent leprosy care for the past six to seven years. Mr. Choi, my official coworker, rarely visited and the provincial mobile team visited the health center in Naju rather than the villages. No wonder so many patients had ulcers and no one had received any eye care.

Mr. Choi, nearing retirement, had a permanent scowl on his face. The first day I arrived in Naju, about a year before, he demanded, "Where is the other volunteer? I have a letter from Peace Corps saying that I was getting two volunteers, a Mr. Ko Seong-cheol and a Mr. Paul Courtright. Which one are you?"

With my three months of Korean language instruction, I was challenged to explain that Mr. Ko and Mr. Paul were one and the same—me. He had little time for me. He had Miss Kim, one of the secretaries, "assigned" to work with me on my Korean language to shorten the painful months of inadequate communication. She'd taken on her task bravely and laughed through my many mistakes and mispronunciations. Miss Kim didn't speak a word of English and saw no reason to learn it. She was working at the health center until she could find a husband. English was not required. Now, I realized that I was grateful that she'd worked hard to reduce the number of times I made a fool of myself.

Copying the records had really improved my written Korean. With these files in hand, I had gone around my village putting names to faces and patient records to individuals. I enjoyed my work, but my social life was pathetic. There was no one around my age in the village. Everyone seemed to be older than forty or younger than ten. Secondary students were sent off to live elsewhere—places where no one knew that their parents were leprosy patients. University students lived in Gwangju. The steadfastness and determination of my patients to make sure that their children led lives untouched by the disease and its stigma amazed me. Still, I had zero social life.

◠　　◠　　◠

The bus crossed the line into Jeonnam Province, and Gwangju was only another forty-five minutes down the road. I felt content with my plans and happy that my backpack was stuffed with books to fill the alone time. I continued to stare out the window at the unchanging landscape—rice paddies, pine forests, small towns. All was good.

In Gwangju, I headed off to buy tinned tuna and other food items for home. I walked to the small store with its narrow rows, tiny shelves, and the ubiquitous cigarette displays. I found no tuna. "*Ajumeoni*, where's the tuna you had a few weeks ago?" I asked.

"Last week some foreigners came in and bought all of it. Why would they buy so many cans of tuna?" she said with a quizzical look.

Oh man, this was not the response I wanted. I sighed as my shoulders sank. "Foreigners like to make sandwiches with the tuna," I said. With a hope that seemed likely misplaced, I asked her, "When will you get some more?"

"Why doesn't your *ajumeoni* buy fish in the market?" she said, unwilling to give up on her disbelief that people would buy canned tuna when fresh tuna was so much better.

"I live in a small village and there is no market nearby," I said, comfortable that the lie would go unquestioned. Men don't cook in Korea, and I was not willing to tell her that I cooked for myself and that cooking fresh tuna was too much hassle.

She continued, oblivious to what I had said. "Only foreigners eat the tinned tuna and there are only a few foreigners here in Gwangju. I can order some more, but you need to buy it."

She was tough. I couldn't promise I'd be her primary market. I was really looking forward to having some tuna even though its price placed it in the category of a luxury good. Sourly, I wondered who the foreigners were— ready to bang on their doors and demand my share. There were three Peace Corps volunteers based in Gwangju, but I doubted it was any of them— they were as cash-strapped as I was. It must have been one of the missionary families. I would not be banging on their doors.

I left the store grumpy. Halfway down the block, a young student caught up with me. I knew what was coming next.

"Hello, my name is Kim Dae-moon. What is your name?" he started. I was to be his English language lesson for the day.

In my grumpiness, I wanted to bite his head off. I resisted the urge. "My name is Paul. What school do you attend?" I responded, to continue his English language lesson.

"Gwangju Middle School. Where are you from?" came the next question. Thus began the start of the twenty questions all middle school students are destined to ask us "round eyes."

"I am from America."

"What is your job?" was question three from him. Hmm. Should I be honest and say that I worked in a leprosy village near here? That would certainly put the conversation to an end quickly.

"I am a Peace Corps Volunteer," I said.

"What are your hobbies?" was question four. Had students been taught to ask the same questions in the same order?

"I like to hike. I like to read. I like to spend time with friends." This was not the time for more complicated or thoughtful English sentences. I laughed inwardly. This kid was not really interested in my responses other than being able to understand what I was saying and to get ready for the next question.

"Do you have any brothers or sisters?"

"I have an older brother. He's in America and helps my parents." I had learned that the second statement was an important addition. As the younger son, I had considerably more freedom than my older sibling. His filial responsibility to take care of our aging parents was clearly prescribed in Korean society. Of course, it also meant that he would inherit the family home and farm—if we had a family farm in Idaho.

"How old are you?"

Asking one's age was usually followed by a list of other questions. If it were an adult asking me the age question, subsequent questions were always the same. "Are you married?" "Not married? Why not?" "Do you smoke?" "No? Why not?" Fortunately, students didn't pursue this line of questioning, so I could answer without a sigh. "I'm twenty-six. How old are you?"

"I'm fourteen years."

I had guessed a bit younger. I found it difficult to estimate ages in Korea.

"Are you married?" he asked. He had a twinkle in his eye. Cheeky little dude. I laughed.

"No, I'm not married."

We rounded the corner and the bus station was just ahead. We should be able to wrap this up quickly.

"Nice to meet you, Kim Dae-moon. I'm going to get my ticket for the bus to Nampyeong. Good luck with school," I said.

"Goodbye, Mr. Paul," he said, only slightly mangling the "l" at the end of my name.

I probably made his day. There were only a handful of foreigners in Gwangju and he'd lucked out in finding one to practice his English with. My grumpiness lifted.

*   *   *

Nampyeong was no more than a cluster of one-story shops and homes with a health post and a police station. The bus stopped just long enough to discharge and pick up passengers, and I had learned that I needed to remind the driver that I was getting off in Nampyeong—otherwise, he might not bother to stop. Nampyeong was hemmed in by the main north-south road from Gwangju to Naju and by the east-west flowing river. For a small part of the way, the river paralleled the dirt road that led to Hohyewon, and I had seen it in every season now. The water level did not change much and it was surprisingly clean.

I walked from the bus stop to where the pavement met dirt. I waved at the shopkeeper who greeted me as I strolled up. "Mr. Ko. How are you?"

None of the Koreans I knew and worked with was aware of my American name. It was as if I had traded in one identity for another. Peace Corps had provided me a Korean name, Ko Seong-cheol, the "Ko" serving as my family name. While the Chinese character for "Ko" meant "tall," there were many taller volunteers and the name selection happened before I arrived in Korea. "Ko" was closest they could get to "Courtright," so there was some logic to the choice.

"I'm well, Mr. Park. How's your family?"

"They are well," he replied as we walked together to the yard between his *gage* and his house to fetch my bicycle. He had allowed me to keep my bike there when I had to travel by bus from Nampyeong. Although his yard space was small, there was a well for water, a clothesline with clean clothes still limp from just being washed, and a vegetable patch.

"Thank you for keeping my bicycle. Did you hear about the demos in Seoul?" I'd waited until we were away from anyone else on the street before I asked.

"Those students were only causing trouble. We heard that they've stopped their demos and are back at university. We don't have time for demos," Mr. Park responded, always practical. Since the death of the policeman was on the news, I was sure he knew about it. He didn't mention it and I wondered if it colored his perspective of the demos.

I was keen to get home, but I took the time to buy a few food items from Mr. Park. Usually, I didn't want most of what he stocked—cigarettes, soda, crackers, and cookies. Even though it was still a bit early in the season, he had some melon and I happily purchased it to take home.

The rutted dirt road that I navigated on my bike, with my day pack strapped to my back and a sack of groceries dangling from the handlebars, demanded my complete concentration. I was tired—tired of the upheaval, tired of being on the road, and tired of the time away from Hohyewon. I was ready to get back to my "real work" and to hunker down in my village.

Guilt had recently become my constant companion. Dad's diagnosis of esophageal cancer and subsequent surgery weighed on me. I'd only returned to Korea a little over one month ago from a couple of weeks in Boise to be with my family for his surgery. My parents wanted me to remain in Boise and take over their tool rental business. They tried not to show their disappointment in my decision to return to Korea. Nonetheless, I couldn't escape the knowledge that they wanted me there.

Lost in thought, I almost ended up in the ditch at the side of the dirt road. I shook myself. The work ahead of me in Hohyewon was going to require a lot of me. In particular, many of my patients had eye conditions that needed treatment. I had learned about the specific eye conditions associated with leprosy and how to diagnose them, but that didn't mean I was qualified to manage them. They needed to be evaluated for surgery or other specialized treatment by an ophthalmologist. My job was to get them the care they needed, and that care was far away from the village.

I rode into Hohyewon—it had not changed. Two large churches, one Catholic and the other Protestant, towered over the predominantly small cinder-block and tin-roofed houses. Each church was large enough for a village twice the size of Hohyewon. Some of the leprosy work in the country was carried out by missionaries and building churches was part of their work. I didn't know a leprosy patient who was Buddhist.

I passed one of the rapidly disappearing packed-mud-and-thatch houses. The mud-and-thatch houses were much warmer in the winter than the newer houses, but they "looked old" and Korea was on the move. The village appeared large for the number of people who lived there. Chicken coops outnumbered the houses and there were at least one hundred chickens for every person. I parked the bike next to the small room where I lived and breathed a sigh of relief. I unlocked the door, took off my shoes, left them propped outside the door, and walked inside. I was home.

Day 4

Saturday, May 17:

Getting back to normal

—

The chickens were creating a racket, and the noxious smell wafting from the coops they called home invaded my room early. A knocking got me up and moving. Still groggy, I opened the door to find my village leader thrusting some papers toward me. "Some letters for you, Mr. Ko."

"Thanks, Mr. Kim," I said, then paused as my head cleared. "I'll come by to see you later about plans for my trip to Suncheon."

He nodded his assent and strode away. A short, trim man in his mid-fifties, Mr. Kim was the most no-nonsense Korean I'd ever met. Conversations were always short, to the point, and devoid of emotion. He intimidated me.

Now I had a choice to make: read the mail or fix some breakfast? The mail won. It amazed me that a few scraps of paper in an envelope with stamps could make its way from a small post office in the mountains of Idaho to my doorstep in tiny Hohyewon. The process was reversed when I wrote letters and, as far as I could tell, they all arrived.

I sat down cross-legged on the floor and opened the letter on top. My Idaho friends' lives had continued in much the same way as before, while mine had undergone a radical change. My work for the US Forest Service in the mountains of central Idaho could not have been more different from my leprosy work in Korea. Most of my friends remained baffled by my decision to come to Korea. I still found it difficult to explain.

With some trepidation, I opened the letter from Mom. It was three weeks old. She said that Dad was doing okay. I managed to push the guilt I was feeling down for a little longer. After a quick bite, I set out to see patients.

Sun Mo-mo was the first patient on my list to visit. Mo-mo was not her real name. She acquired leprosy as a young woman, left home, and had changed her name decades ago to protect her family from the stigma of the disease. Now, she lived with her daughter's family in a small cinder-block house. It had a little wooden porch, under which shoes were kept. I added my shoes to the lineup, hunched down to enter the house, and sat cross-legged on the floor with her, her daughter, and her six-year-old granddaughter. Mo-mo was about sixty years old but looked over seventy, mainly because she was stooped from osteoporosis. She had lagophthalmos—the muscles in her lower eyelid had wasted, her lower lids had collapsed, and she could not close her eyes completely. She needed eyelid surgery to prevent blindness. She agreed to have surgery but was afraid to travel to the hospital.

"I've not been out of Hohyewon in over ten years. I could get lost."

"I'll be with you for the bus rides to Suncheon," I reassured her. "You'll have surgery on Tuesday. Park Sung-moon and Cheong Ko-sun will also be going with us, and they'll come back with you on Wednesday or Thursday."

"Oh, you'll not stay with us?" she said almost in a whisper.

"No, I have to come back to Hohyewon Monday afternoon." Waiting around the hospital until they were all discharged did not appeal to me. I respected the work that the hospital did, but the Christian proselytizing made me feel uncomfortable—why couldn't people do good in the world without wrapping it up in religion?

Mo-mo gazed down at her lap. "I'll wait until you can go with me and bring me back."

That was the response I'd feared. Besides her lagophthalmos, which was severe and attention-grabbing, she'd lost most of her fingers over the forty years she had lived with leprosy. Lack of sensation, nerve damage, and injuries, all untreated over many years, had left her as the stereotype for the stigma associated with leprosy. Could I blame her for not wanting to bear the looks on people's faces?

"I understand. I'll arrange another time to take you." I'd need to find something else to do in Suncheon to avoid hanging around the hospital. I knew that there were a number of other patients who would also find it difficult to travel. "I'll ask the doctor if she can come here to do the surgery—or maybe Naju." Although it sounded like an easy solution, I knew it was not. It seemed that a lot of my work was as a logistician—get patients here, get surgeons there, get supplies for the care of ulcers, get drugs from the health center to the village, and on and on.

I put my shoes back on and walked to the other side of the village, near the Catholic church. There, Mr. Park and Mr. Cheong, with a couple of other men, were putting eggs into large racks for transport. We talked while they stacked up racks. They both said they were ready to go for surgery. Their lagophthalmos was not as severe as Sun Mo-mo's and their other disabilities were minor. I gave them a list of instructions I had written out laboriously the night before. I sometimes found it easier to write out instructions in Korean than to say them—particularly when people responded with a thick Jeonnam accent. I reminded them, "I'll take you, but you'll have to come back by yourselves."

"Who'll pay for the bus fare?" asked Mr. Park.

"I'll pay for the bus to Suncheon. I'll give you money for the bus fares back. Be sure to bring a change of clothes." Both must have been outside the village before and were not overly concerned. "Your surgery will be done by an eye doctor from Norway who works in Suncheon. You remember her from when she visited here a few months ago?" I said, reminding them of the visit I'd organized. She'd confirmed the cases I'd prescreened and we had a schedule to take them to Suncheon, a few at a time.

"Oh yes. We remember her," Mr. Cheong answered without hesitation. I was probably the first foreigner to step foot in Hohyewon and she might have been the second.

"Good. Monday morning I'll meet you at the office at seven. We'll get the seven-fifteen bus to Nampyeong, then Gwangju."

I glanced down. There was a large bulge in Mr. Park's right sock that looked like a bandage over an ulcer. "What happened to your foot, Mr. Park?"

"Eh?" He glanced down to where I was pointing and sheepishly pulled a slightly crumpled cigarette pack from his sock.

I laughed. Christian missionaries had hammered home that drinking and smoking were not Christian characteristics. Mr. Park had found a way to hide one sin. It was certainly better than an ulcer that needed management. He laughed with me and we shook hands before I left for my next patient. I made it a habit to shake hands with leprosy patients, particularly when I was around those who didn't have the disease. I might have little impact on their medical condition, but maybe I could help reduce the stigma people faced.

My next patient was a youngish man undergoing a leprosy-related reaction. He lived in a tiny one-room mud-and-thatch house in the middle of the village. He was recently diagnosed, his wife had left him, and he had no place to go. He came to Hohyewon just before I went to Boise. His limbs were swollen and hot to the touch, and I had referred him to the provincial leprosy unit. I hadn't had a chance to create a record on him yet. I knocked on his door. "*Yeoboseyo*," I called out.

He answered in a reedy but welcoming voice. I opened the door, sat on the threshold of the doorway, and took off my shoes, leaving them propped next to the hardened mud wall. A single bulb hung from the ceiling, itself only two meters high. It gave off little light, as it was coated with dust.

"How are you feeling?" I asked him.

My eyes were still adjusting to the dim light and he was sitting against the wall, out of good view. He slid forward. I breathed a sigh of relief. His reaction had subsided—the swelling of his limbs had reduced. I touched his arms and legs—he was no longer hot to the touch.

"I went to the hospital in Gwangju. They gave me some medicines," he said, as he pulled out a half-sheet of newspaper that encased three small white envelopes. "I still have some pain, but it's not as bad." The slight smile on his face was a welcome sight.

I did a thorough examination of his hands and feet and was relieved that he had not developed any ulcers. I finished and sat back.

"Thanks," he said. I was puzzled. I wondered why he was thanking me. All I had done was to encourage him to go to the hospital for treatment. He continued. "It helped me think that you, an American, wanted to help me. You're not afraid."

"It's okay," I stammered, not knowing what else to say. After a few seconds, I bid my farewell and slipped my shoes back on. I was still worried about the young man. He had no family, was in a strange village, and now was cut off from much of society. He had a tough road ahead.

My last stop for the day was at an isolated house about ten minutes' walk from the village. Mr. Choi could barely walk, had little ability to use his hands, and was blind. On top of all of that, he had aggressive skin cancer on his face that had nothing to do with his leprosy. Incredibly, he was always kind and welcoming, even though there was little I could do to help him. I had arranged an appointment at a hospital about three hours away to address his cancer and I would take him next month. Getting him there was going to be rough.

His wife always tried to give me food. They were dirt-poor, living in a small earthen-walled-and-thatch house. My living situation, opportunity, health, and wealth felt almost obscene. I gently refused her offers. She was always grateful whenever I came and if I was not careful, I would find a few sweet potatoes that she'd sneaked into my day pack. Today was no different. "I'm sorry I've not come to see you in a while," I said in honorific Korean.

Mr. Choi responded, "Mr. Ko, don't worry," adding, "How's your father?"

His wife must have seen my discomfort, so before I could respond she intervened.

"Your older brother is there to care for him. That's good." They were always interested in my family and had heard many of our stories.

"Yes, my older brother is with my parents."

We talked about the upcoming trip to the hospital. I cleaned and rebandaged an ulcer on Mr. Choi's foot and reminded him to soak the foot before putting on a new bandage. It was getting on five in the afternoon and after a full day in which I spoke only Korean, I was exhausted. I walked slowly back to my room. Work in Hohyewon was good—it gave me a sense of purpose.

Back to my room, with shoes neatly propped outside the door and patient records neatly stacked inside, I put on some music. A knock at the door and the gentle voice of Mrs. Moon reminded me that I had forgotten to give her my clothes to wash that morning. I gathered them up and opened the door to find her holding a bowl of steaming rice, with a lid keeping it warm. "We've not seen you for a long time, Mr. Ko."

"Oh, thank you," I said, and dropped the clothes to accept the rice. "Yes, I'm sorry. I'm happy to be back." I scooped up the clothes and clumsily handed them over to her. She wrinkled her nose with a look of mild disgust at their smell. I quickly added, "There were demos in Seoul and tear gas smells really bad." She quickly retreated with the smelly bundle. I wrapped the bowl of rice in a towel to keep it warm. The smell of the rice made me hungry, and I dug into the large bag of sweet potatoes and sliced one. Fried, with the rice and some peanuts, it was perfect. I was in heaven.

During cooking and eating, a Jackson Browne cassette tape played and I was transported to another place and time. I wasn't discontented—in fact, Jackson Browne helped ground me in the here and now. I glanced around the room that contained my entire life: paperbacks piled in one corner, clothes stacked in another, a little hot plate on a low table under the window, and my sleeping mats rolled up along one wall. It amazed me to think that I could live in such a small place with only a few changes of clothes and some music tapes. I was content.

Day 5

Sunday, May 18:

Disturbing rumors streak across the sky

—

Wow, the whole day off! It had been ages since I had a day off. I tried to finesse a leisurely breakfast of fried eggs on toast but found it tricky on my single burner. Toasting and frying could not be done simultaneously.

I was looking forward to the day. I'd hike, write letters, read, and clean up my one-room house. The last came first and, given its size and simplicity, took only twenty minutes.

I packed a sandwich, filled up a canteen, grabbed my boots, camera, and day pack, and stepped out into the soothing morning air. My plan was to explore the hills and ridge that separated Hohyewon from Gwangju. The bells at the two churches rang in competition as I made my way out of the village and along the embankments of rice paddies across the road. When I moved into Hohyewon the residents were disappointed that I didn't attend church. Most people wanting to practice their English included a question about my religious affiliation somewhere in the middle of the "twenty questions." It was a question I still struggled to answer without causing consternation. Religion was a form of identity in Korea but not one that meant anything to me.

I timed my escape with the pealing of the bells since that meant that all of the kids were at church. No one would be running after me asking where I was going—alone. There was no literal translation of the word "privacy" in Korean and I was hopeless in trying to explain why I enjoyed hiking alone.

I made my way across some rice paddies and considered jogging but quickly discarded the idea. Jogging along the ridges between the rice paddies would likely lead to a sprained ankle and being face-deep in rice shoots. My pace was leisurely. After about twenty minutes I came to the river. I crossed it using a bridge that might have been around since the Japanese occupation. It was functional and sturdy. On the other side, I gazed up and around to assess the best way to reach the ridgeline. The range of high hills separating me from Gwangju was covered in pines, some now over twenty-five years old. As I squinted, I could see patches of tidy rows of the trees. They toyed with my eyes and brain until I remembered that they were probably planted as part of the recovery from the destruction of the Korean War. With the exception of the trees around some old temples, it was hard to find a tree older than the war. I flashed back to a regret I had early in my time in Korea—I had not brought my binoculars with me. What an idiot!

Today's hike was new. I started uphill along a small yet serviceable path, not quite sure it led up to the ridgetop. At least I was heading uphill, in the general direction I intended. That was good enough for me. After about thirty minutes I came upon a tomb. Neatly tended grass surrounded the manicured mound. Small butterflies flitted through the warm rays of the sun and cicadas chirped in the still air. Graceful pines, with new bright green needles emerging from tips, edged the area and a couple of large brown-glazed clay pots were lying in the thicker grass at the edge of the clearing. I suspected that the clay pots contained ashes of deceased relatives. There was no marking showing who was buried here, but the well-tended grass suggested that markings were unnecessary. I skirted the edge of the clearing, not wanting to disturb the residents, who could have been in the ground for hundreds of years.

The small trail led upward and after another hour or so I came upon a second tomb, this one not quite as well-tended. I found a spot in the clearing where the sun could warm my back, so I sat down to enjoy my sandwich. There was not a cloud in the sky. The only sounds that reached the residents of this mound were from the throats of birds and the wings of cicadas.

I glanced up and estimated that the ridgetop was still another hour away. There was plenty of time. My pace slowed as the steepness increased and the forest thickened. My views disappeared in the dense forest. I continued uphill, comfortable but not overconfident in my direction—that was good enough for me. I looked forward to having a good panoramic view at the top, with Gwangju on one side and Naju County on the other.

I reached the ridgeline. There was nothing to see except trees and more trees. Gwangju was not visible, nor was Naju, nor my home. The forest was too thick—what a disappointment! Without a view, there was little reason to stay. Within fifteen minutes I retraced my steps on the path back to the nearest tomb. There, as I napped, the sun penetrated my T-shirt to remind me that the world spun no matter where I happened to be. The birds and bugs kept me company, their sounds different, yet equally comforting.

In the late afternoon, I wound my way back home, grateful for the serenity of the day. Tired but satisfied with the day spent hiking, I slowly ambled up to my room. Mr. Kim was waiting for me outside my door. His presence, on a Sunday afternoon, surprised me. His compact frame seemed more tense than usual and the look on his face was grim. I stiffened, thinking, he's one tough character. Before I could offer my greetings, he spoke. "Mr. Ko, did you hear the news? There have been demos in Gwangju."

"No, I didn't hear. I've been hiking all day," I said, perplexed, my head tilted to one side.

"Something bad happened in Gwangju today," he said. "It's not safe to go there."

He was standing stiffly and his brow was creased. He leaned slightly in my direction, not challenging but anxious. Although I sometimes had difficulty "reading" him, I could tell that he was upset. This was an emotion I'd never seen in him before.

"You're taking Mr. Park, Mr. Cheong, and Mrs. Sun to Suncheon, right?" he asked. His rigid stance and furrowed brow did not change.

"Yes, in the morning," I said. "I'm only taking Mr. Park and Mr. Cheong. Mrs. Sun doesn't want to go. We'll get a bus to Suncheon from the Gwangju bus station in the morning." He and I both knew that the only way to get to Suncheon was through Gwangju. The look on his face didn't change.

"Okay, be careful," continued Mr. Kim, as he shifted his weight from one foot to the other and cast a glance into the distance, toward Gwangju. "There have been demos and some people have been killed. Martial law has been declared."

My mind raced. Oh shit! Not again! Should I cancel the trip to Suncheon? I thought for a few seconds. Demos would be near the university or in the middle of town, rather than at the bus station. I decided not to cancel and gave him a look with as much confidence as I could muster. "I'll be careful. I'll come back tomorrow night and Mr. Park and Mr. Cheong will return on Wednesday or Thursday." How dangerous could it be anyway?

Mr. Kim and I didn't agree on many things, but he was fiercely loyal to the residents of Hohyewon. He entrusted me to keep them safe. After a few seconds, he stared me straight in the eye, nodded his farewell, and strode off. I was uneasy.

I understood the concept of *nunchi*, which loosely translated to "reading the eyes," but found applying it to Mr. Kim particularly challenging. In some situations in Korea, words masked the real intention of the speaker. In complicated or sensitive situations, I was always trying to assess the speaker's *nunchi*. On a number of occasions, by observing the speaker's eyes I found it possible to interpret the spoken "yes" to actually mean "no." Understanding *nunchi* made uncomfortable situations more manageable. This was why wearing sunglasses could be considered rude, and I always took off my sunglasses when I was talking.

○　　○　　○

Inside my room I sat on the floor cross-legged and started a letter to a friend, taking the opportunity to sort through my thoughts. I was confused. The words of Mr. Kim, although few in number, were at odds with the day I had just spent. I looked back at what I had written. My friend from Forest Service work in Idaho would appreciate my account of the hike, so I added something about that. I veered off-track quickly and described the demos in Seoul—and what I had just heard about Gwangju. My letter made Korea sound like two entirely different countries. To some Idaho friends, the image of Korea continued to be that from *M*A*S*H*. I found it difficult to describe a dynamic country founded on traditional values—there were many, many contradictions that I had yet to come to grips with.

There was a soft knock at the door. I opened it and Mrs. Moon handed over clean dry clothes—the warm sun today had done the trick. I paid her and went back to writing. In order to get letters, I had to write letters, so I didn't view writing as a chore.

After I fixed my meal, I got ready for the morning trip. I had enough cash for the expected expenses. My day pack was ready with a paperback, dictionary, change of clothes, and toothbrush. I replayed the short conversation with Mr. Kim. I didn't remember him talking about student demos, just demos—odd. For him to refer to Gwangju as being "dangerous" worried me.

My impressions of Gwangju had changed as I got to know it better. I had two Peace Corps friends in Gwangju. Tim, who had arrived in Korea a year before me, had come out to my village to help me iron out a few problems with Mr. Kim—his Korean language being light-years ahead of mine. He was last out to Hohyewon about four months ago to help me visit a few patients who needed ulcer care. It snowed heavily that January day and we had laughed at the thought that, before becoming Peace Corps Volunteers, we imagined that we would be sweltering in some tropical rain forest or baking in some desert hamlet, rather than freezing our butts off in Korea.

I'd stayed with Tim and the Korean family he lived with many times on my way through Gwangju. He had a wide circle of Korean friends, mostly from the university, and I was happy to tag along. Gwangju was becoming my home away from home. There was no bathing facility in my village, so I used a bathhouse near the Gwangju bus station. Best of all, Gwangju had great food—even if tuna was difficult to find. In centuries past Gwangju was known for its gangsters, rowdiness, and fantastic food. Both the gangsters and the rowdiness had become history, but the food was still considered some of the best in Korea. As far as we were concerned, there was no better.

Day 6

Monday, May 19:

Something awful happened here

—

Our bus pulled into the Gwangju bus station. Mr. Park and Mr. Cheong, both dressed in traditional *hanbok*, got off and I followed. There were about twenty buses parked in a row facing one side of the building. Their final destinations were listed in large letters on the windshields as well as on the signs marking their parking bays. The smell of roasted garlic hung in the air. It was early enough that the air was still cool.

We walked into the nondescript two-story building to get tickets for Suncheon and stopped in our tracks, almost falling into each other. The air inside was charged with tension. There were soldiers everywhere. They looked like mannequins cut from the same mold—I couldn't tell one from another. Camouflage uniform, helmet, sunglasses. They acted as if they owned every molecule of breathing space within shouting distance. The charged air made sweat bead on my brow and neck. What the hell was going on?

I glanced around at the other travelers in the large open space. Their faces exhibited a range of emotions—mostly fear, but I also detected hatred and disgust. No one, including me, made eye contact with the soldiers. The fear that emanated from the crowd started to infect me. I moved to buy our tickets so we could get out of there as quickly as possible.

With tickets in hand, I turned around from the ticket counter to give Mr. Park and Mr. Cheong their tickets and saw their mouths slightly agape. I looked around to see what transfixed them. Two soldiers, their stances threatening, were challenging a young man near the buses. Their menacing tone and raised clubs were at odds with the youth's bowed head. With every word that the soldiers shouted, the young man appeared to shrink. The soldiers appeared to be only a few years older than the youth. Within a few years, he would be part of the same military. Conscription was universal and all Korean men had to do up to two years of military service. Just a few months ago, these three might have been lounging as friends, drinking *soju*, and laughing.

People going in and out of the bus station gave the soldiers a wide berth. My patients seemed to be more tuned into the mood than I and grew more afraid. "Mr. Ko, we must go now."

We turned toward the Suncheon bus. It was only a few footsteps away, but before my feet made contact with the bus steps, there were some loud thumps and a woman's voice pierced the air. "They're killing him! They're killing him!"

Everyone froze. We turned around. The young man was on the ground, unmoving. Blood pooled beside his head. The soldiers stood over him, their posture still threatening. One soldier turned and faced us. There was no movement or words coming from the stunned crowd. "Leave the area! Now!" barked the soldier.

I remained rooted to the spot; my patients stood just behind me. I couldn't think. I couldn't move. I couldn't make sense of what had just happened. Mr. Park gave me a gentle nudge to get on the bus. My mind reeled. My whole body was numbed. I moved sluggishly and took my seat; the sight of the young man and the woman's cry shook me to the core.

In front of me, a woman sobbed quietly. Mr. Park and Mr. Cheong, seated across the aisle from me, stared straight ahead, not looking at me or at each other. The door closed. Not one word was spoken as the bus

left the station. All eyes rested on laps or were glued to the windows—
it appeared that everyone was in shock. What prompted these soldiers
to treat a fellow Korean citizen that way? What actually happened in
Gwangju yesterday?

Our bus worked its way through the outskirts of Gwangju. The city
appeared calm and peaceful. I couldn't get the image of the young man out
of my head. His head was bowed and I only saw the soft profile of a young
face. He had offered no resistance. Next, he was prone on the ground, beaten
and broken by the soldiers. Was he dead?

The insulated security of the bus and the receding city failed to shake
the images from my mind. I tried to focus on the forested hills, verdant rice
paddies, and small bustling towns to soothe my frayed nerves. Every once in
a while I glanced furtively at my fellow passengers. I was afraid to look them
in the eye—afraid that their *nunchi* would reveal torment and horror.

The ninety minutes to Suncheon could have been twenty-four hours or it
could have been ten minutes. Time stood still and time sped up. I watched
everyone get off the bus. A shocked stare remained on every single face. The
world had changed for all of us. Mr. Park, Mr. Cheong, and I had not shared
a word since Gwangju. When I glanced at them they averted their eyes.
Were they embarrassed to acknowledge what had happened or how they
felt?

Thirty minutes and another short bus ride later we walked into the hospital.
The two men were registered and took a seat on the hard wooden benches
in the waiting room. I ambled off to the eye clinic. In the short time it took
to get to the clinic I decided that I wasn't going to talk about Gwangju with
the doctor; instead, I was just going to focus on work. The clinic door was
open, but no one was around. The doctor must have just stepped out for a
few minutes. I went in and got set up to examine patients. Over the last six
months, I'd spent every Monday morning that I could at the eye clinic to
learn how to use the equipment to examine eyes, what to look for, and what

the management options were. The doctor had me examine every patient at the slit lamp before her as well as give my findings.

"Oh, Paul. Good to see you," Dr. Topple said as she closed the door behind her. Mia Topple was a Norwegian missionary doctor and my teacher.

"Hi, Dr. Topple. I brought two patients for lid surgery," I said.

"Great. Shall we get started?"

With a nod, I picked up the chart on top, stepped out the door, and called the first patient's name. An elderly woman, very much like Sun Mo-mo, stood up and hobbled inside. I seated her at the slit lamp and did my exam, then stood up for Dr. Topple to do the same as I described my examination findings. This process went on nonstop for the next two hours until all of the waiting patients were seen. Dr. Topple agreed that both Mr. Park and Mr. Cheong needed surgery, and she scheduled them for the next day. I was so engrossed in the work that my mind didn't stray to the young man lying in a pool of blood in Gwangju.

But the moment the work was done, the memory of the morning flooded back. I bid farewell and bolted out of the hospital. I went along the same dirt road I had used to get here to find Erik, a Peace Corps Volunteer who worked at the hospital. Erik's small house was just off the road, one of a group of residences for hospital staff. I called out "*yeoboseyo*," and Erik opened the door. He invited me in, but he didn't have a chance to say more than "hi."

"Erik! What's going on in Gwangju? I just came from there and it was nuts. A young guy was clubbed right in front of me as I was getting on my bus. A couple of soldiers probably killed him! I can't believe it. What the hell's going on?" All of the tension erupted, the words tumbled, and my voice went up an octave as I struggled to maintain control. Since the words came out in one breath, now I had to pause. I still stood in the doorway, my shoes still on. I squatted, kicked them off as if they were a hindrance, and went inside. Erik's place was about twice the size of mine, but it contained the same high windows, waxed paper floor, a burner in one corner and sleeping mats in another. He had a small refrigerator—a bit of luxury. He went over, reached in, and got a few items to make sandwiches.

"You didn't hear? There was a demo in Gwangju. Students marched, carrying banners demanding that Chun Doo-hwan resign and that Kim Dae-jung be released," Erik told me as he went to the small sink and washed a couple of glasses.

"Kim was arrested?" I asked. "What for?"

"Martial law was declared Saturday night. Then Kim was arrested. Why? Who knows? Then all hell broke loose. I was with Tim near the university on Sunday," Erik explained, his own voice starting to rise.

"What's going on with all of the soldiers? When I was in Seoul the demos were being managed by the police. I didn't see any police in Gwangju," I said, as I struggled to maintain composure. I couldn't grasp the image of Koreans killing other Koreans.

"We heard that Chun sent in soldiers from Gyeongnam, knowing they would be loyal to him," said Erik, referring to the province to the east of us.

"What happened?" I asked as I sat on the floor.

"Tim and I were out near the university. Students and other people were gathering in the street and, after a while, they started to march toward the provincial office. Police and soldiers blocked the way. The students stopped and some threw rocks," he said, as he focused on the ceiling and tried to remain calm. "Then the soldiers charged. Everyone scattered. The students, people on the sidewalk, everyone took off running. It was total chaos. Tim and I ran into a *gage*. It soon filled up with bystanders and students. Three soldiers came in. They grabbed students and started beating the hell out of 'em with their clubs. Tim jumped between the students and soldiers and started yelling at the soldiers to stop. I couldn't believe it—the soldiers actually stopped. I guess they didn't expect to see a foreigner. Tim and I then dragged the injured students to the back of the *gage*. We spent the next few hours carrying people to the hospital. Students were killed! We saw others taken away by the soldiers. It scared the hell out of us." Erik went silent, still gripping the glasses. I leaned forward, stunned, my mouth half-open.

"Does anyone outside of Gwangju know about this?" I asked, recalling that the death of the policeman in Seoul was on the radio, TV, and newspapers within an hour of the event. I had not seen or heard any mention of Gwangju on any media this morning.

"I dunno. There's been nothing on the news about it," Erik said, his shoulders sagging. "I think some people here heard about it, but no one is talking about it."

He opened some Spam, sliced it, spread some mayonnaise on a couple of pieces of bread, and repeated the steps. We ate in silence. His description of Tim getting between some soldiers and students unsettled me. Should I have tried to protect the young man outside the Gwangju bus station? Was I a coward?

"What's going to happen next?" I asked.

"Beats me, but from what you just told me, it sounds like it's getting worse, not better."

We finished our sandwiches and looked at each other with a mix of anger, horror, and confusion. I leaned forward, my elbows resting on my legs. "Thanks for the lunch, Erik. Would you mind checking on Mr. Park and Mr. Cheong tomorrow? I brought them from Hohyewon. They're having lag surgery tomorrow morning," I said, grateful to talk about something else.

"Sure, I'll check on them," Erik replied. "What're your plans?"

"Oh man, I don't know. I need to get back to my village today," I said. "I have no idea what else to do." There was no reason to stay here at the hospital. Within a few minutes, I said goodbye, laced up my shoes, and retraced my steps of the morning. That meant the bus back to Suncheon and another one to Gwangju. The entire way I tried, but failed, to come to grips with the question: what should I have done in Gwangju this morning?

Dusk was fast approaching as the bus wheezed into Gwangju. It had been a long day and I was exhausted. I wanted to sleep during the ride but couldn't. The bus was not crowded—just twenty people or so.

We were about five minutes from the bus station when, almost simultaneously, I said, "Oh shit!" and the driver said, "*Ayegomay!*"—the Korean equivalent of my exclamation. He hit the brakes.

A block ahead of us fire consumed a city bus and a couple of taxis, all bunched together like some children's toys. The debris all over the road was only visible through the darkness when flames rose and provided some light. It had started to drizzle, giving the scene an even more ominous cast. Farther in the distance, other vehicles burned.

The bus windows were closed and we couldn't hear anything. It was like watching a silent movie. Every passenger was now up, nervously pressed against the windows, craning to see what was happening. The streets ahead were deserted. There was not a moving bus or car in sight. The driver pulled the bus over to the side of the road and cut the engine. We were a kilometer away from the bus station.

"Everyone out. I'm not going any farther. Get home quickly!" he shouted as he turned around to face us.

The door opened and, at once, the sound of distant gunfire startled all of the passengers. People piled off quickly and were swallowed up by the dark, damp streets. The driver and I were the last ones off.

"Do you have a place to go?" he asked.

"Yes, I'm fine," was my somewhat untruthful response. The idea that I might get back to Hohyewon tonight was out of the question. The driver didn't bother to lock up the bus before he took off, away from the burning vehicles. I strode off to Tim's place, which happened to be in the direction of the burning vehicles. Sidewalk tiles and stones littered the ground and in the deepening darkness, I tried to balance walking as fast as possible with as carefully as possible. I tripped on a piece of sidewalk tile but caught myself. All of the bus stop canopies had been ripped off. Every *gage* was closed up tight and no streetlights illuminated the scene. It was as if the town had collectively decided that being open and being outside would invite danger and destruction. Who or what had caused this? It took me about fifteen minutes to reach Tim's place, my heart high up in my throat as I pounded the pavement. Time passed in a blur.

The *ajumeoni* finally came out in response to my persistent knocking on the metal gate. I was afraid to call out loudly. She opened the gate and hustled me inside. "It's not safe out there," she said, admonishing me.

I put my shoes next to the neat row of footwear at the front door. There were a lot of shoes stacked up for a house where only three people lived. I walked into the main room. The tension was palpable. The *ajumeoni's* son, Ok-jin, and three other college students sat on the floor with Tim and Judi, the other Peace Corps Volunteer who worked in Gwangju. Tim looked gaunt and tired.

"What the hell's going on?" I asked. I dropped my day pack and joined them on the floor.

Tim sighed. "Yesterday was a massacre. Chun had his soldiers attack anyone demonstrating. Young, old, it didn't matter. I don't know how many people were killed. Some people said that it was more than a hundred."

"Oh my God. I was with Erik in Suncheon today. He told me about you guys in the *gage*. You were lucky the soldiers didn't go after you."

"I think the soldiers were surprised to see a 'round eye.' They didn't know what to do."

The gate clanged and we jumped. The *ajumeoni* went out. We were all silent, trying to pick up the voices, too soft for us to understand. Collectively, we held our breaths. The gate, which needed oil, creaked open. The *ajumeoni's* eldest daughter, recently married and living near the university, came in, breathing fast and quite shaken. "The soldiers are going house to house searching for students. Some are being taken away. Others are being beaten. We need to hide Ok-jin."

Everyone looked at each other, not quite sure what to do. Tim stood up, gazing at Judi and me. "I need a favor."

"Sure," we both responded and got up, confused.

Tim grabbed his day pack and turned to us. "Can you stay here and protect Ok-jin and his friends? I need to go to another student's house and spend the night there. If they're rounding up students they'll probably target his house. He's been involved with the demos."

"Sure," Judi and I said in concert. We regarded each other and knew that we could not fight off any soldiers. Our only weapon was being a "round eye."

Tim left without another word, as did the older sister, each to seek a different destination but with similar objectives in mind. The small household remained tense but was quieter. Some heads were bowed. I wondered what had they seen.

Judi, Ok-jin, and I huddled. "If soldiers come to the gate and force their way in, it'll be Paul and I that they will face," said Judi.

"Agreed," I concurred, and Ok-jin nodded his head in affirmation. "Where can you hide?" I asked Ok-jin.

"It is probably best if we go up on the roof. There are stairs in the back," he said. Judi and I could offer no better suggestion.

Everyone in the room, each of us in our own way, was in uncharted territory. We sat in uncomfortable silence. Ok-jin's friends had said nothing since I arrived. Where were their families? The fact that they were here suggested that they were not in Gwangju and they'd had nowhere else to go.

Ok-jin's mother brought in a small table with a plate of melon slices— each slice was perfectly arranged on the plate with a toothpick sticking out of it. Politely, each of us reached out and took a slice without saying a word. The simple act of being served melon slices brought a sense of normalcy to the room.

The sound of gunshots and yelling outside made us jump. Normality had been erased. Judi and I stood up expecting to hear pounding on the gate. Everyone else watched each other but didn't move. The gunfire stopped. The yelling stopped. There was no pounding on the gate.

The *ajumeoni* got out extra sleeping pads and the sleeping arrangements were made. Judi would sleep with the *ajumeoni* while Ok-jin, the other students, and I would use two mats in the room where Ok-jin and Tim usually slept. Over the past year, I had learned to surrender any sense of "personal space." I was now sleeping with a bunch of guys with zero space between us. There was a small chamber pot in the corner if we needed it, the latrine being outside the house. We all undressed, hanging our clothes on hooks on the wall. With so many bodies in the room and a single small window near the ceiling, it was going to be a warm night. Ok-jin's mother had offered food when I arrived, but I'd gone through the etiquette dance of saying "I have eaten" three times before she stopped asking. We all knew our roles. Now I wished I'd accepted her offer.

Day 7

Tuesday, May 20:

Getting marching orders and the last bus home

—

No soldiers pounded on the gate overnight. Tim showed up in the morning in time for some rice, kimchi, and seaweed soup. He related that all was quiet where he had spent the night. "What do you have planned for today?" he asked.

"I need to get back to Hohyewon, but I also want to hit the post office," I said. Then I remembered that the post office was near the center of town— the site of the upheavals.

"You sure? Who knows what might happen today," cautioned Tim.

"Yeah, but it seems that the military has a pretty tight grip. People are afraid. What more can happen?" I knew that Tim was far more knowledgeable about the situation than I was, but I felt confident that I was not a target.

"A lot," said Tim, unsettling me.

Judi said that she was going back to her home on the other side of town. We all went out of the front gate and headed our separate ways. Tim walked to the hospital where he worked. I was off to the post office. Ok-jin and the other students stayed behind. His mother had been adamant; they were not to leave the house today.

The streets were still wet; the dampness had suppressed many sounds and it was surprisingly quiet as I made my way. I saw people hesitantly poke their heads out of gates and doors. Were they trying to decide if it was safe to go about the day's work? I crossed to the other side of the main street—most shops were still closed. Then I looked ahead. Menacing and scary tanks lined the road. Had I made a stupid mistake to venture into town? Was I being a voyeur?

I picked up my pace and reached the relatively small downtown area in fifteen minutes. Few people were on the sidewalks and no buses or taxis were visible. Only a handful of motorbikes and bicycles, weaving around the debris, tentatively crossed the usually crowded streets.

Armored personnel carriers and tanks clustered at intersections—intimidating enough on their own, but even more ominous with soldiers milling about. A bulldozer pushed aside the burned-out husks of a bus and taxi. A few shopkeepers cleaned the area in front of their shops. The saplings that lined the sidewalk appeared scrawny and forlorn, as if they had witnessed something that no one should have seen.

I walked on and stepped over the broken sidewalk tiles, stones, and glass that covered much of the pavement and sidewalks. Shopkeepers glanced up occasionally, probably trying to make sure that no trouble was brewing. There was not a single young person to be seen—every Korean here had to be at least forty years of age. This was a school day and schoolchildren should have been marching off to class in their starched uniforms. There were no schoolchildren.

Everything was wrong with the scene. Schools were closed. Buses were not running. Taxi drivers were not hustling for passengers. More than all of these physical activities, there was an eerie sense of foreboding in the air.

I stopped and scanned the scene. Was anger the overriding sentiment or was it fear? On the main street with few civilians, but many soldiers, it was impossible to know. Had the harsh tactics of the soldiers on Sunday and Monday beaten the town into submission?

On the main road, near the provincial office, I gave the soldiers a wide berth. They were numerous and threatening, and I slowed my pace. With my head down, only my black hair showed, so I kept it up to avoid being mistaken for a Korean university student. If visible, my black mustache and my other facial features screamed "round eye."

I saw that the massive armored personnel carriers, intimidating as hell to me, could not fit down the narrow side streets. Most of the soldiers clustered around the carriers. Maybe they were seeking the protection of the metal.

I turned into the small walking street, closed to most traffic, near the post office and felt as if I'd walked into a little enclave. On this and the other small streets, people seemed to be going about their daily lives. Shopkeepers, office workers, police, and post office staff made the best of a bad situation. The people on the side streets were not as many as on a typical Tuesday morning and the demographics were skewed to the upper ages. Still, the scenes here suggested that Gwangju was trying to work today.

The next street I took led to the post office, its front door up a few steps from the corner where two small streets met. Here, the atmosphere was different—anger, instead of fear, dominated. My own emotions had also evolved. I didn't fear for my own safety, but I started to fear for the situation I was walking into. Like virtually every person I saw on the street, I was angry. Tensions were on the rise and events could spiral out of control. That scared me.

I knew of the demands of university students and of the anger that was unleashed when those demands were ignored. Not just ignored, but disparaged and attacked. On these small side streets, the demands and anger came from an unexpected source—from *halmeoni* and *ajumeoni*—people considered unwavering and hardworking in traditional Korean society. They didn't express their anger by throwing sidewalk tile or rocks. It was evident in the grim and determined way they went about their work, combined with the occasional calls at the soldiers down the block. A *halmeoni* near me shouted "shame on you" at the soldiers as she walked into a *gage*. I wanted to give her a big hug.

I approached the post office, a large single-story redbrick building that was built during the Japanese occupation. There were a few steps up to the front double doors. Off to one side, I saw a crowd of about twenty people, an amorphous, unorganized group from all walks of life. They started jeering as a group. "Shame on you!" they called, followed by other taunts including "Down with Chun Doo-hwan!" "Release Kim Dae-jung!" and "Murderers!"

I felt safe in this crowd. The military was hunting down students, not *halmeoni* and shopkeepers, and certainly not foreigners.

I mounted the steps into the post office and went straight to a counter to get stamps. It felt good to be cocooned by the cool, quiet interior. Everyone was going about their business as if what was underway outside was a world away. The counter staff were mostly young women probably happy to have jobs until they got married.

The young postal worker let me look through the available stamps, and I chose enough for my letter and a few extras for the next couple of letters. She handed over the stamps and I handed over the cash. I stepped away from the counter and licked the stamps I needed, stuck them to the envelope, and dropped it into the post box.

Wham! A tear gas canister flew through a window behind me. Glass shards scattered everywhere. Screams were followed by the pounding of feet as everyone tried to escape the rapidly expanding blanket of tear gas.

I slung my pack on my shoulder and dashed out the front door. Why the hell would they tear-gas a post office? A torrent of people spilled out the front door, scattering in all directions. My safe cocoon had vanished.

A whiff of tear gas seeped from the front door of the post office, but most of it was trapped inside. Standing at the top of the steps, I paused to figure out my next move. I shelved my plan to stop by the store and see if tuna had come in. It was time to go home!

Below me, on the street, a policeman was surrounded by a diverse group, young women from the post office, shopkeepers, and *ajumeoni*. I listened in.

"What's going on?" a person asked. "You're supposed to protect us."

The policeman shrugged. "I don't know what's happening. We weren't told that the soldiers were coming here."

"Why are they doing this to us? Why have they killed our students?" pleaded an *ajumeoni*, her waving hands splattered with garlic.

The policeman, looking just as angry and upset as the small crowd, reiterated what he had said before. "These are soldiers from Gyeongnam. We're also shocked by what happened on Sunday and Monday. We were home with our families when the soldiers started attacking."

"What can we do?" demanded an older man standing next to him.

"There'll probably be more trouble. Go home. Make sure young people stay inside and protect them," he said.

He bowed slightly out of respect for the elders in the crowd. There seemed to be no hostility directed at him. Before the small crowd dissipated, each person made his or her own small bow and formal farewell. It struck me that this was the proper relationship between the people and the government.

Down the street, the military remained in place and the taunts continued. The post office continued to trap most of the tear gas and the air outside was less noxious. I walked down the redbrick steps and ventured across the small street. Midway, a *halmeoni*, dressed in a slightly worn but still serviceable bright pink and lime-green *hanbok*, grabbed my arm. I assumed that she needed help to cross the street. She was less than 150 centimeters in height, slight, and bent over. Her grip, however, was firm. She faced me and peered directly in my eyes.

"Are you an American?"

"Yes."

"Have you seen what happened?"

I felt as if an electric shock had been sent through my entire body. "Yes. I'm sorry," I stammered.

She did not let go.

"We'll have to be sorry later. Now, you must be our voice," she said as she pointed at my chest. "Koreans have no voice. The world doesn't know what our soldiers are doing. But you, an American, can make sure people hear about us. You have to speak for us," she commanded me.

I stood there, rooted to the spot, my mouth agape. The seriousness of what I had witnessed crashed down on me. I was involved, like it or not. I was afraid to look her in the eye, but her grip and the force of her voice wrapped themselves around my inner turmoil. I had to gaze at her.

"I'll try," I faltered, silently berating myself for my pathetic response. But her fierce eyes and steady grip told me that she wasn't asking. She was demanding this responsibility from me. I was to witness the events and let others know. She released me.

"You must tell our story," she stated again. Out of respect, I bowed. She turned and walked with determination, her bent frame slightly less bent, into a nearby *gage*.

I couldn't move. It was all mind-boggling. I blinked a couple of times and took a breath. Slowly, I took stock, first of myself, then of the shrinking space around me. Normally-respectful citizens cursed the troops. The street leading to the provincial office building was blocked off and soldiers did not allow anyone to pass. The tension increased with each second. As with any fire, the fuel was plentiful, the oxygen too. All that was needed was a spark. Damn, I needed to get out.

I glanced across the street to where the *halmeoni* had gone, still reeling from the responsibility she had put on my shoulders.

I turned left, southward toward the bus station. Each small street led to another. Soldiers stood in groups on the larger streets, mostly to my right, never too far from their armored vehicles. The noise on the main street grew and I wondered what was happening. I wasn't willing to venture from the safe confines of the small streets.

"Shame!" and "Go!" echoed down the streets, wherever soldiers were. There seemed to be a growing momentum; anger had replaced fear and defiance had replaced anger.

I wove my way through the warren of back streets. It took longer, but I felt safer. I couldn't see what was going on out on the main roads and that suited me just fine. I was still shaken from the tension downtown. After many twists and turns, I was across from the bus station. There was no torn-up sidewalk tile nor rock littering the ground. There was also no one under thirty years of age. I had managed to avoid soldiers since leaving the post office. Here, I could not. They were positioned all around the bus station. I had to face them and cross their lines to get into the station.

I pushed through a small crowd who faced off some soldiers. Arrogance seemed to seep from every pore on their uniformed bodies and they acted as if these people—their own people—were annoying flies. Alienating university students was one thing—angering *halmeoni* was quite another.

I crossed and stepped inside the bus station. I heard the sound of a few rocks hitting the pavement and turned around to peek out the large windows. Unconsciously, I held my breath and waited. I exhaled when I didn't hear any gunfire. The people doing the most shouting were quickly surrounded by soldiers, separating them from the rest of the crowd. It looked like they were being intimidated, but no truncheons were employed. Within a few minutes, the overwhelming military force had people scattered and the protest dissipated.

It was almost four o'clock and the bus to Nampyeong was filling up. I bought my ticket and dropped heavily into a seat at the back of the bus. I had been a bundle of nerves for the last nine hours. I gazed out the window while I waited for the bus engine to turn over. My body started to melt into the seat. I felt as if every nerve ending in my body had switched off. I was cocooned again and heading home.

Day 8

Wednesday, May 21:

You can push people only so far

—

I woke disoriented. What a lousy night's sleep! The chopping sound of helicopters, grinding gears of large vehicles, and some man-made beams of light that had disrupted the usual nighttime peace and quiet of Hohyewon appeared to have come from a section of the Gwangju–Naju road that opened out into a fairly flat section of countryside. Some years ago, the government, concerned about the possibility of North Korean invasion, had constructed a particularly wide section of road there to make it an emergency landing strip.

I shook my head. Were the helicopters just a dream? If not, what the heck had happened? I rummaged around for some aspirin to tackle my headache.

My little burner was doing triple duty this morning: boiling water for coffee, then eggs, and finally water for a sponge bath. The well and pump where I got water were outside and I was in the habit of filling a container the night before. Now, I felt more energized than when I first woke, so I gathered up my supplies, including bandages, ointment, and patient records, to start my rounds. I opened the door to find Mr. Kim and three other village officials waiting for me in the warming sun.

"Mr. Ko, we were worried about you," said Mr. Kim. "Did Mr. Park and Mr. Cheong make it to Suncheon?"

"Yes, they'll have their surgery today and will return later this week." It was calming to be talking about work.

Mr. Kim, his face pensive, took the lead and switched the topic.

"We heard that many people in Gwangju were killed on Sunday. Is that true?"

"Yes, that's true. There were soldiers from Gyeongnam in Gwangju. They killed many people, mostly university students. People are very angry," I said, as my voice started to rise. There was little hope of keeping my emotions completely in check. I suppose my rigid stance, clenched fists, and voice gave off messages of their own.

One of the other leaders, whose name escaped me at the moment, stepped toward me. His haunted eyes, uneasy stance, and shuffling feet made me feel ill at ease.

"There are no buses today. And our phone isn't working," he said in a subdued voice. There was only one phone in the village, and it was in the village office. If it didn't work, we were cut off. He nodded toward the men on his left. "Mr. Shin here has a daughter and Mr. Nam has two sons at Jeonnam University in Gwangju. They've not heard from them. My son is also at Jeonnam. There are a few other families that have children at schools in Gwangju. They're quite worried," he said.

Images of the young man unmoving on the pavement outside the bus station rose in my mind. Was that only Monday? It seemed like weeks ago. Were there scenes of distraught parents, like these men, being played out in villages throughout Jeonnam Province? Out of respect and worry, I bowed my head.

"I'm sorry," I said. It was all I could muster.

"Are you going back to Gwangju today?" asked Mr. Kim. I jerked my head up.

I had a Korean language class scheduled for Saturday in Masan and I'd considered traveling the next day. I did some calculations: if I went to Gwangju today, then I could continue on to Masan the following day.

"I was going to go to Masan tomorrow. But, I could go to Gwangju today, then get the Masan bus tomorrow," I said.

There was a look of relief on their faces. They had a side discussion, way too fast for me to keep up. They nodded together and Mr. Kim turned back to me.

"We'll get you a list of students in Gwangju. Call them when you get there," he said. It sounded like a curt demand, but the pained looks on the faces of the men around him told me how worried they were about their sons and daughters.

"Didn't you say that the phone isn't working?" I asked, puzzled that I was being asked to call when the village phone didn't work.

"Yes, but the phones might be working within Gwangju," said Mr. Kim.

I couldn't think of much else to add. My plans to visit some patients today were shelved. The men seemed anxious to be off. "I can leave for Nampyeong in about forty-five minutes. Would that be enough time to collect the names and phone numbers?"

They all nodded and then scattered in different directions.

I retreated inside my room and put away my supplies. I folded up my sleeping mats and grabbed my day pack, some clothes, a toothbrush, and a camera. Then I sat down for a minute to think. What the hell was I doing, trying to go to Gwangju? Something happened in Gwangju late yesterday and last night. That "something" was probably not good. Was this a smart thing to do?

A knock on the door startled me. I opened it to find Mr. Kim holding a sheet of notebook paper. He put it into my hand. There were six names and six phone numbers. He and I bowed slightly to each other.

"I'll be back on Sunday after my language class," I said.

As I stepped outside I glanced over at my bicycle. I decided not to take it. I locked my door, put on my shoes, and started to walk. The dirt road was little different underfoot today compared to being under my bicycle tires a few days ago. There were the same ruts created by the last rainstorm, which made travel on it difficult. Thick foliage on the edge of the road quickly gave way to rice fields to the south and hills to the north. Birds bounced among the branches of the trees that lined the south side of the road, making a racket. Were they telling me *don't be an idiot*?

The sound of a motorcycle from some village past Hohyewon caught my attention. I flagged the rider down and hopped on the back. My day pack was heavy, but I was glad to have my camera. I had been annoyed with myself for not taking it with me to Suncheon the day before. The motorcyclist let it rip and I almost tumbled off the back. I gripped the seat underneath me and tightened my thighs.

Nampyeong is the first small town after leaving Gwangju heading south. Gwangju is the big city and lush green hills separate it from Nampyeong. Naju, farther south, was a decent-sized town. The land between Nampyeong and Naju was flat and carpeted with rice paddies—except for the considerably long and wide section of the road from which I thought that the sounds emanated last night. Every time I passed through Nampyeong I marveled at the roaring business of small *yeogwans*, hole-in-the-wall restaurants, vehicle repair shops, *gage*, and of course brothels. Nampyeong served the transport industry—in all sorts of ways. The small town was never going to appear in a tourist guide. Any mention of it was likely to include the word "rough."

I hopped off the motorbike next to Mr. Park's *gage*, where I usually kept my bike. It was closed. He once told me that his *gage* never closed during daylight hours. Yet, now it was locked up tight. I continued toward the main road. Along the way, I saw only a few people and all of the small shops were shuttered. In the distance, up at the main road, things appeared quite different. The intersection was packed with people. There seemed to be more people milling around in the intersection than lived in Nampyeong.

As I reached the intersection, I was even more impressed at the number of people. Along the main road of one-story shops, there wasn't a bus, truck, or car to be seen. Almost all of the shops were shut. Koreans never closed their shops in the middle of the day—some family member would always step in when needed. On the street where buses normally disgorged and sucked up passengers there were no vehicles.

I was baffled. There were multiple small groups of people engaged in boisterous conversations. Instead of the usual stares I got, now I was ignored. There was a group of about ten people near the bus stop and I joined them as I rummaged for my dictionary. Everyone was talking way too fast. Added to that, their heightened emotions and Jeonnam dialect meant that I struggled to understand the thread of the conversation. I felt like an idiot.

Bit by bit, my ear started to pick up some of the discussion. They were talking about Gwangju, but not just Gwangju. They were talking about things that had happened in Naju, and even farther south in the seaport of Mokpo. What struck me even more than the words they spoke was *how* they spoke them—typical Korean formality and reserve had been abandoned. The words, the gestures, and the way people interacted indicated that something momentous had happened in these places. Everyone, young and old, was excited, some even joyous.

Yesterday I had seen fear, anger, and defiance. Now, just eighteen hours later, I was seeing elation. The mood had shifted beyond my comprehension. What the hell was going on?

The sound of an approaching bus startled me. It was coming from Gwangju rather than going the direction I needed. Still, I thought, at least the buses were running. As it neared, the crowd in the street parted and let out a cheer to welcome it. A large banner proclaiming "Release Kim Dae-jung" sagged on the front grillwork. All of the windows were broken out and the occupants, mostly young, happily chanted and banged sticks, ball bats, and metal rods against the side. Incredible!

Kim Dae-jung was the favorite son of Jeonnam and was the most well-known opposition figure. Years ago, when he was a political exile in Japan, the Korean government had kidnapped him there, brought him back to Korea, and imprisoned him. He'd been released last year but, in the last few days, jailed once again. His demand for democratic reform had galvanized students across the country, particularly here in Jeonnam. The military feared his influence and decided that it was best to rearrest him.

The residents of Nampyeong, *gage* owners, mechanics, hookers, and *ajumeoni*, all let out a massive cheer when the bus stopped. Everyone on the street, old and middle-aged alike, was as enthusiastic as the young men and women on the bus. A couple of *halmeoni* in threadbare *hanbok* started dancing together. An electric current running through the young people on the bus galvanized the crowd in the street, and me as well. We were light-headed, almost euphoric. This gritty little town seemed like the center of the universe.

The bus only stopped for a couple of minutes, then continued down the road to Naju. I stepped back, glanced down, and took a long breath to gather my thoughts. I looked back up to see a police van, the type that had been set on fire in Seoul, barreling toward us. Everyone cheered! Were they crazy? Shouldn't we sprint for cover? As it slowed, the red paint on the front became readable. There were some unfamiliar Korean characters referring to Chun Doo-hwan. Flipping through the pages of my dictionary, as fast as I could, I learned a new Korean phrase: "Draw and Quarter Chun Doo-hwan." What a relief! This was not a vehicle bristling with weaponry and soldiers intent on rounding up people.

Two young men and a young woman who stood next to me introduced themselves and, in excited voices, described the events of the previous night in Gwangju and Naju.

"We did it! We kicked the bastards out!"

"What? The military is no longer in Gwangju?" I asked, still trying to come to grips with the scene and its implications.

"Most of Gwangju—they still hold the provincial capital and train station, but the rest of Gwangju is free. We heard that they've left Naju, Mokpo, Hwasun—they left late yesterday," one of them responded excitedly with the names of other small towns in our province. This was their moment and they were giddy with delight.

"It started yesterday afternoon," explained the young woman with obvious satisfaction. "People were fed up. The bus drivers and taxi drivers led the way. They created a barrier, protecting people, and some rammed the military vehicles."

I was trying to picture any kind of spontaneous collective action by bus and taxi drivers, neither known for their political rebelliousness. Taxi drivers, in particular, were usually independent and freewheeling. It was hard to envision them joining forces with bus drivers.

"Were many people killed?" I asked, although I dreaded the answer.

"Some, from what we've heard—but not many," the young woman answered, her voice hesitant and her eyes downcast.

"The bus and taxi drivers used their vehicles to ram the military lines," said one of the young men. "Now, the military will have no choice—they'll have to leave the provincial office."

"Really? What happened in Naju and other towns?" I asked.

The other young man took a step forward. "I'm from Naju. We heard what was happening in Gwangju. Everyone gathered near the train station. There were no soldiers in Naju, so no one was hurt. But the large police headquarters was burned." He paused to catch his breath and then said, "It seems that the same thing has been happening everywhere south of Gwangju."

"So, this area in Jeonnam is not under military control? And the people are now in charge?" I asked, with my hands, palms up, as I sought understanding.

Their eyes lit up. "Yes! No more soldiers!" the young woman nearly shouted.

"Wow!" I said in a loud voice in English. My new friends immediately grasped what I meant.

All of the groups around us seemed to be having similar discussions, each with their own spin or interpretation or bias. Groups ebbed and flowed, and it was impossible to ignore the enthusiasm. This was uncharted territory for everyone.

"As you can see, everyone's happy," the young woman added, her excitement contagious as she swung her arms to take in the entire scene. How right she was.

The crowd started to move slowly south to an intersection a short block away, where the police station stood. I went with the flow. The police station looked forlorn, its door locked and no police around. The crowd swelled and an argument broke out between two men near the front. They were talking way too fast for me to understand.

"What are they saying?" I asked.

My newfound friends' eyes were glued to the scene and one of the young men responded, although transfixed by the argument.

"They're arguing about the armory in the police station."

A burly middle-aged man walked past the two. With a loud crack, he broke the lock on the front door. It crumpled under the force of his massive wrench. He flung the door open. A handful of men rushed into the small structure. On the street, the two men continued to argue, but events overtook the argument. Men started bringing guns and ammunition out.

Shit! My heart lurched. The Korean military had not planned on a rebellious public. All Korean men undergo military training and are quite handy using rifles. Not only did the handful of men who entered the police station know how to use the weapons stored there, but every single man on the street did too.

The focus of the military, of the police, and of the intelligence branches had been on one single foe for the last twenty-seven years—North Korea. I thought back to the rumors that the Gyeongnam paratroopers were told that North Korean elements were at play in the uprising in the city. It struck me that everyone around me would take up weapons against "the North" if there was a threat. Today they cheered the rout of their own military. The farmers, shopkeepers, and drivers on this rural street were a potent force that demanded justice. Their own government had let them down. Not only that, their government had attacked and killed their brothers and sisters. Now they were ready to fight back.

My young friends declined to take a weapon. "We cannot shoot at our soldiers," one of them said. His friends agreed, although reluctantly.

"How do we protect ourselves?" asked the young woman.

"Has anything like the killing of civilians by the military ever happened in America?" the youngest-looking man asked me.

I paused and thought for a few seconds before I responded.

"Yes, about ten years ago soldiers shot a number of university students."

"Really?" he responded, his brow creased and mouth open in disbelief.

"It was at Kent State University. Students were protesting against the Vietnam War."

"What happened after the shooting?" the woman asked, appearing upset with the answer I had just given.

"I really don't know. Everyone was really angry that it happened. I don't know what happened to the soldiers or their leaders," I said, embarrassed to admit this.

Within a few minutes, the multitude of reactions in the crowd crystalized into two: those advocating that guns were, unfortunately, necessary for defense and those rejecting their use for fear of retaliation by the military. Everyone was animated in a way that I'd never experienced in Korea. Regardless of which faction they fell into, the words and faces around me emanated the same message—look what we've achieved!

No more guns and ammunition came out of the armory—it had been stripped bare. Some weapons were piled on the road. Some were held by residents. Some were handed to people in the battered buses still trundling through town.

There was no shouting, but passions were running high. The crowd grew to well over two hundred. A military jeep with four civilians pulled up at the edge of the crowd. Two got out and waded into the crowd—their demeanor suggested that they commanded some authority and people stepped aside to let them through. As one man reached the center of action, he peered at the small pile of weapons.

"Return the guns. If you keep the guns it'll only give the military an excuse to retaliate—and to kill again," he said in a low but commanding voice.

The crowd quieted. After a few seconds, I heard voices in the crowd—

most in agreement. One by one, people started to hand forward their guns. An old man grabbed a gun from the pile and stopped them. "If we return the guns they can be used against us. Break them!" he shouted.

In a flash, the somber mood became joyous again. Young and old snatched rifles that had piled up in the street. They gripped the rifle barrels and gleefully smashed the stocks in the street. Wood shattered and flew in every direction. A new pile started to form, this one of metal parts— scratched, bent, and now completely unusable. My friends joined in the righteous destruction. After a few minutes, they came back to stand with me, their flushed faces beaming with satisfaction. A ripple of fulfillment ran through the throng as the final rifles were destroyed. The whole process, from the time the armory was opened until the arsenal was destroyed, had taken less than an hour.

The men got back in their jeep and continued south to Naju. People cheered them, then started drifting off. There was a sense of accomplishment on the faces of people around me. I could imagine them saying, "Maybe I didn't make any money to feed my family today, but I witnessed a wonderful event and I contributed to its success." The pile of metal and wood remained in the street, a memorial to a day like no other.

"Where are you going?" one of the young men asked me.

"Well, I was planning to take a bus to Gwangju today," was my hesitant response. My plan to get a bus to Masan seemed unlikely.

"You can ride in one of the buses with the students," he suggested, adding, "We'll help you."

"No, that would be wrong," I said, unable to come up with the Korean word for "inappropriate."

They were ready to help, but I could imagine how a photograph of me in a bus with a banner that demanded an end to martial law or to have Chun Doo-hwan drawn and quartered would go down with the Peace Corps. Not a good idea. The intricacies of how to explain that I needed to "behave" was beyond my language capacity.

"Can you help me get a ride on a motorbike or car?" I asked.

One of the young men flagged down a motorcyclist heading in the direction of Gwangju. He was willing to give me a ride most of the way. Unlike the requisitioned buses and military vehicles that careened along the road, he had no banners on his motorbike. More importantly, he controlled whatever maniac driving tendencies he might have possessed. At a fairly sedate speed, we passed vehicles that had been abandoned—maybe they ran out of petrol or developed mechanical problems? We passed a police station that was about the same size as the one in Nampyeong. It had been torched. Farmers, men and women both, stood on the side of the road and cheered passing vehicles—even us. I waved back. The scene that unrolled in front of me didn't fit the military's narrative about "riotous students and hoodlums and North Korean influence." This was rural Korea. There were no students here. Most were, in fact, elderly farmers!

The motorcyclist turned off about a kilometer before Gwangju. I hopped off, thanked him, and started walking. It was relatively peaceful and quiet. There were no soldiers. I did wonder who was in charge, if not the military. In this little corner of Korea, the military government had retreated. My newfound friends in Nampyeong gave me the impression that the military had withdrawn from an even larger area. That larger area could include the entire province or even more. Without phone contact, I couldn't find out what was going on. I didn't even know if Chun was still calling the shots or not.

My thoughts were interrupted by the throbbing of an approaching helicopter. I gazed up, unsure whether I should hide. Its military markings answered my question. The military, and most likely Chun, was still in charge. It continued toward Gwangju.

As I neared the unmarked boundary between urban Gwangju and rural Jeonnam, the blaring sounds of an unplanned uprising replaced the tranquility of rustling poplar and ginkgo in the countryside behind me. A large military truck sat crumpled, on top of the small guard station, next to the railroad tracks. The truck smoldered, an occasional flame flickering up in search of fuel.

There was a cacophony of buses, trucks, and all forms of menacing military vehicles clustered at the petrol station. They waited impatiently to suck up its life-giving juice. Replenished, they roared out.

The reluctance to distribute weapons I saw in Nampyeong was replaced by a freewheeling gift-giving in guns here. Guns were handed from vehicle to vehicle and from person to person. The large number of weapons, even though they appeared fairly basic, made me nervous. I wasn't ready to wade into the scene.

I sank into a plastic chair outside a *gage* near the petrol station to drink a lukewarm Coke. I tried to make sense of everything going on in front of me. I didn't know where many of the vehicles, some lumbering and some racing past, were coming from or going to. There was no money changing hands at the petrol station. For today the petrol was free. That was not going to last long.

I finished my Coke and handed the bottle and some change to the *ajumeoni*. Petrol might be free, but not Cokes. It was getting on toward five o'clock and I had to make a decision. Should I try to continue deeper into Gwangju proper or should I go back home? If I continued into Gwangju I'd have to walk to Tim's house. There were no buses or taxis on the roads. I was not going to hitch a ride with the students in one of the military vehicles or buses. From what I'd heard, there were a couple of places in Gwangju that the military still held. That meant conflict.

I struggled to maintain my emotional distance from the rapidly unfolding events. Somewhere, deep in my core, the horror of the killings by the soldiers and now the excitement of their overthrow had turned me into an enthusiast of the uprising. It was time to right a wrong. Still, if I were to remain in Korea, I knew that my outward appearance needed to be different. I had to remain an impartial observer.

I stood up and slung my day pack over my shoulder. Rifle fire split the air and I jumped. The *ajumeoni* let out a small scream and I dropped to the ground. I glanced up and over my shoulder and realized that the shots were fired into the air in celebration. With an apologetic grimace, I got up. That cemented my decision—I was going home. I picked out some biscuits to sustain me. The frightened *ajumeoni* who took my one-hundred-won coins for the biscuits for the ride home confirmed that my decision was the right one.

"We heard that the military is going to return tonight. They'll kill many people," she said, shaking and almost dropping the coins I had just handed her.

"I'm sorry," I said as my shoulders sagged. It was emotionally hard to say those two simple words. All I could offer her were words. Her downturned mouth matched mine and I could see my mother's eyes in hers—deep opaque pools that had seen tragedy and knew there was more to come.

I turned and trudged back toward the road to Nampyeong and Naju. There were still a few working vehicles on the road, getting on with day-to-day life. I was grateful when a small pickup truck, partially piled with cartons of cigarettes for Nampyeong and places farther south, pulled over. I climbed in the back and settled myself among the boxes. Farmers who had lined the road earlier had gone home. There were few people out. Even though I passed the same rustling gingkos and serene rice fields I'd seen on the way into town, my mind was not soothed.

Nampyeong was quiet. The streets had been cleaned. The broken rifles were no longer piled up in the street. It appeared that people had retreated to their homes for evening meals and time with family. Most *gage* remained closed, including Mr. Park's. Today's events were now a part of its history. How would it be remembered? The solitary walk back to Hohyewon gave me more time to think. I had no idea what was going on or what would happen next. I couldn't seek guidance from the Peace Corps as the phone lines were cut. I wasn't even sure what I would tell them.

Oh my God, I'd completely forgotten to try to find a phone at the *gage* to call the students in Gwangju! The list of names and phone numbers was burning a hole in my day pack. As I neared Hohyewon I made a plan. Tomorrow morning I would cycle to Naju. I'd take the back roads, the shorter route. In Naju, I'd go to my health center and see if they could call the Peace Corps in Seoul. And, if Seoul couldn't be reached by phone, then I'd head to

Gwangju.

I reached Hohyewon in the fading light, exhausted and hungry. The thought of facing Mr. Kim with my failure to make the calls weighed on me. It'd be much easier to just lie than explain what had happened. I knew I couldn't fail the second time.

The sugar rush from the Coke and the biscuits had worn off. I splurged, making a three-egg omelet with a side of boiled sweet potato for dinner. Dire Straits blasted on the cassette player. The music transported me back to my small apartment in Boise. I searched for but couldn't find any guidance from my past life in Idaho.

I ached to talk to someone in English. The best I could do was write a letter to a buddy, to make sense of the day. I wrote but soon realized I still couldn't make sense of everything that I had seen, heard, or felt. All I could do was recount it. That would have to do. I finished the letter, then found an envelope and some of the stamps that I'd bought just a couple of days ago. As I licked the stamps, the taste of the glue brought me back to the tear gas and the chaos outside the post office. The *halmeoni* was facing me again, keen that I tell the story of how people were being brutalized by the military. How things had changed since then!

I kept one part of my promise to the *halmeoni*. I sat on the floor and started to write again. I wrote and wrote and wrote. My ache to converse in English returned. I really wanted another perspective. What had my eyes, my ears, and my other senses missed? I turned over the Dire Straits cassette. My mind drifted.

Day 9

Thursday, May 22:
The mundane and the crazy can easily coexist
in the middle of an uprising

—

The drone of the swarm of helicopters was deafening. What time was it anyway? My eyelids were heavy and my vision was blurry as I sat up and glanced at my alarm clock. It was two in the morning. I shook my head, confused. Other sounds intruded. The roaring engines of large trucks or other vehicles obliterated the usual Hohyewon nighttime sounds of chickens and a few dogs. Without turning on the overhead light, I stumbled around and grabbed a T-shirt and shorts. I opened the door, fumbled for flip-flops, and stepped outside. It felt like I was reliving the previous night. The sounds came from the exact same area. What the hell? This was the place I would pass through on my way to Naju in about seven hours.

The military was up to something. Maybe they were moving completely out of Jeonnam. Or maybe they were moving back in. My shoulders sagged from confusion and tiredness and a growing sense of fear for the residents of Gwangju. I stepped back inside and crawled back onto my sleeping mats. There were only about four hours till dawn and I wanted every single hour for sleep.

Dawn was quiet and I had no idea when the noise had stopped. Maybe I'd dreamed of the sounds from the middle of the night. At the village office, I found Mr. Kim.

"Greetings, Mr. Kim. I didn't make it into Gwangju yesterday, so I couldn't call any of the students," I said. He nodded.

"Did you hear the helicopters last night? We heard that the military has returned," he said, his voice uncertain. He glanced at the day pack slung over my shoulder. "Where are you going?"

"I'm going to Naju to the health center. I'll try to call the Peace Corps in Seoul from there," I said. Mr. Kim always made me feel uncomfortable. He was short, but he was a force to reckon with. He had led the village to become economically prosperous. Hohyewon's egg production, collection, and marketing was a collective enterprise and he was a skilled negotiator. Every morning, a truck pulled into the village, was loaded with eggs, and was sent on its way. I still struggled to gain his approval. I had nothing to offer to the economic well-being of Hohyewon. We didn't have the perfect relationship and the tension was heightened by the fact that he felt responsible for me. It wouldn't look good if his crazy "round eye" got into trouble. I shuffled my feet for a few seconds.

"Mr. Ko, you must be very careful. We don't know what happened last night, but it's probably not a good sign," he said. I didn't know the Korean word for "sign," but the context made his message clear—something bad had happened.

"I'll be careful," I said as I shifted my weight back and forth, ready to go. I said a quick goodbye, turned, stepped out of the office, strode back to my room, grabbed my bike, slung on my pack, and pedaled out of the village. I had a particular sense of mission—I needed to know what was going on, what I should do, and how I could help. In Hohyewon, I felt isolated and helpless.

The pack weighed about the same as yesterday even though I had switched out my camera for a couple of changes of clothes, a toothbrush, and toothpaste. As always, my dictionary was packed within easy reach. The day before I'd only taken a few pictures, afraid that if I had photos of people smashing guns on the street the military could, sooner or later, use the pictures to arrest people. I also grabbed my pocket notebook. It included all of the new words and phrases that entered my lexicon each day in Korea. In the last week, I'd added a range of new Korean words: for "uprising," "impure elements," and "draw and quarter." The writing was small and cramped and the notebook was nearly full.

The shortcut to Naju was a favorite of mine and, as I left the village, I looked forward to the series of small pathways among the rice paddies. The thirty-centimeter-wide ridge between the paddies was just enough to walk on. The ridges demanded my full attention even though I walked my bike. The breaks between fields to let water flow from one to another were a challenge. I risked a sprained ankle if I didn't step or leap well from one side to the other. More than one Peace Corps Volunteer had to sheepishly report that he or she had stumbled face-first into a rice paddy while trying to take a shortcut.

I kept my head down to keep an eye on each and every step. Quicker than I imagined, however, I was at the small dirt road leading to the pavement. I could ride again. Within ten minutes I was on the pavement, in the area where the noise that had shattered my sleep had come from. This morning Sanpo-myeon was quiet. The roadway was clear and gave no indication of what might have happened last night. The only other people on the road were on old, clunker bicycles like mine. The huge expanse of pavement stretched north and south as well as west. The total lack of evidence of whatever happened here during the night was perplexing.

I stood next to my bicycle for a couple of minutes, took in the scene, soaked up the sun, and tried to match the unreal serenity with what I imagined was going on here only six or so hours ago. A middle-aged man with a younger woman on the back of his bike veered toward me.

"Want a fuck?" she called out.

"Ah… no," I choked out. My eyes widened and my jaw scraped the pavement.

With a laugh, she and the man peeled off and headed toward another man farther along the road. Small, seedy red-light districts were found in almost every town. I'd never been propositioned in the middle of a road, however. I shook my head in disbelief as they continued on their way.

The rest of the ten-kilometer ride into Naju was pleasant. The sun was on my face, the air was clear and crisp, and the flat road made for an easy ride. I crossed the bridge into town. I rode more slowly; this was a very different Naju. The large police station stood blackened and empty. The streets were clean but ghostly quiet. The small police stand on the street corner near my health center was a pile of rubble. No one was on the streets. There were no banged-up buses carrying students or crowds reveling in their victory over the military. There was no suggestion of an uprising. No joyous celebration. Something had changed overnight.

The health center, just ahead, appeared no different. I popped out my kickstand and left my bike out front. The bottom floor was the clinic where there were usually plenty of mothers with their infants attending the antenatal services. Today it was empty. I'd not spent any time in the ground-floor clinics, primarily because there was no special leprosy clinic. This surprised me when I arrived here about a year ago. Naju County had over one thousand leprosy patients, so I figured there'd be a clinic for them. I'd since learned that no patient would walk into a room with a sign over the door saying "Leprosy Clinic."

I walked upstairs and found my coworkers. Almost immediately they surrounded me and told me everything that had happened in Naju, a backwater compared to Gwangju. Naju high school students and others had marched in town and were joined by students and others from Gwangju. The police stations were torched and the small military contingent had pulled out.

"We're really proud of our students," said one of the supervisors.

"Was anyone hurt?" I asked, unsure if the military had reacted as they did in Gwangju.

"No, not like Gwangju," he said, confirming that he knew of the massacre there.

"What happened last night in Sanpo?" I asked.

"We don't know. What'd you see?" asked the supervisor.

"Actually, nothing, but I heard a lot of noise."

"Well, we heard that last night the military flew in a large number of troops," he said.

"I thought I heard trucks too," I said.

"Yes, some military trucks came through Naju too. We aren't sure where they came from," the TB worker said.

"Where are the soldiers?" I asked.

"We don't know," responded the TB worker. "Everyone is afraid to be out. We are keeping young people inside."

Our conversation did not answer any of my questions. They were just as unsure about what was going on as I was.

"Are the phones working?" I asked.

"No," said the supervisor, as five coworkers shook their heads in unison. Calling Seoul was out of the question. I took a breath and let it out slowly. I wanted to let the Peace Corps know what I'd seen and heard and to find out what was going on elsewhere in the country. I also wanted some guidance.

"Are you going to Gwangju?" asked Mr. Park, the county leprosy worker.

"Yes, I'm going to Gwangju," I responded, expressing far more confidence than I felt. There was a sharp intake of breath by a couple of my coworkers. Mr. Park and one of the supervisors regarded each other.

"Please be careful," said the supervisor, his brow creased with concern.

"I will."

"Miss Kim is in Gwangju," said Mr. Park.

This was the same Miss Kim who worked to get my Korean language up to snuff—at least so we could have some reasonable communication. Even after language training by the Peace Corps, daily usage of Korean without a word of English, and the help of Miss Kim, I was constantly humbled by the fact that I still had a long way to go. The daily embarrassments couldn't be helped.

I went down the stairs, swung my pack on, and climbed back on my bike. I pointed it down the same road I had navigated earlier to get to the health center and pedaled with determination toward Nampyeong, and ultimately, Gwangju. I crossed the same bridge, went through the Sanpo area again, and on toward Nampyeong. I didn't stop in Nampyeong to see what had transpired there since last night—I was determined to get to Gwangju before dusk.

●　　●　　●

Midday, I started the slog uphill with only an occasional cyclist for company. The day was getting hot and the uphill grind on my single-speed bike made the going tough. My head was down, focused on laboring uphill. After a few minutes, I realized that I was alone.

I rounded a bend in the road, glanced up, yelped, swerved, and almost tumbled off the bike. Hunched in the ditch beside the road, just three meters away, were five or six soldiers, each with a rifle pointed directly at me. I regained my balance and tried to regain my composure. I was too startled to utter a word. I sat up straighter on the bike and my legs continued to work the pedals, if for no other reason than to keep moving forward. There was no time to think. My goal was to get away from the soldiers as quickly as possible. Sweat dripped down my spine, my shirt was wet, and my heart pounded. I ignored my tired legs. If the soldiers said anything, I didn't hear it.

I struggled to figure out my options as I kept moving forward, my body glued to the bike. I was afraid to cast a glance back. After a hundred meters, my heart rate slowed but sweat continued to run down my spine. I started to count the revolutions of my pedals to calm myself. I stared ahead—a roadblock loomed. A green taxi and a military truck faced each other in the middle of the road. No vehicle could go around them, but a bicycle could. I neared the roadblock and saw that bullet holes peppered both vehicles. Windows were shot out. My eyes widened in disbelief and my heart rate surged again. I weaved my bike around them, afraid of what I might find on the other side.

But there was nothing on the other side. What had happened to the people who were in the taxi and truck? Soldiers would not shoot at empty vehicles. Where had these vehicles and their occupants been ambushed? Had the bodies been taken somewhere? Had this scene played out on other roads leading into Gwangju? My mind whirled as I pushed on through.

I kept my head up. I wanted no more surprises. Up ahead, at the crest of the hill, I could see a real roadblock. Not only were there more vehicles, filled with bullet holes, but four soldiers stood next to them. Go forward or turn around and go back? I had to keep going forward. I felt completely alone.

The four soldiers that stood next to the vehicles, rifles across their chest, seemed more surprised to see me than I was to see them. Their identical crisp uniforms and aviator sunglasses stole their identities—they were faceless. I hated them. My hatred was only a few days old—ever since I saw the bludgeoned young man at the Gwangju bus station. This was not a time to stop and ask questions or to challenge them. I kept the same pace and without uttering a word, I weaved around them. It was as if they didn't exist. I owned the road, not them.

My heart pounded as much from fear as from the exertion. I was grateful to be on my bike. Although it was old and wobbly, it had propelled me around the roadblock and away from the soldiers. I didn't look back.

I crested the hill and started to gain a bit of speed. The farther I got from the military roadblock, the more my bike produced in me an unwarranted sense of invulnerability.

Gwangju was still about ten kilometers away. Were there more soldiers in the bushes yet to come? It didn't matter. I had dictated my intentions to my legs and we weren't going to stop for anything or anyone. I knew I was being watched. I also knew that it was more than just pairs of eyes that were trained on me, but there was nothing I could do about it. If the military stopped me, I'd play the "I don't speak Korean" game.

Around the next bend in the road, the scene altered. There were two large city buses, a minibus, and a private car askew on the road. They were still adorned with white banners, which now hung lifeless. Dozens of bullet holes punctured the vehicles. I braked and slowed to a crawl. There wasn't one pane of glass left untouched and there was blood everywhere. My stomach turned and my mouth went dry. I wanted to scream. There was complete silence except for my labored breath. My chest tightened further.

Oh my God. These were the same buses that joyous young people traveled in on this road yesterday. Late yesterday, I sat in the back of a pickup truck surrounded by cartons of cigarettes and passed by this exact spot! Maybe I saw this very bus go by as I was sitting in the back.

I stopped, let my bike fall over, and sat, cross-legged, in the middle of the road. I let my head drop between my knees. I thought I might pass out. Although my eyes were closed, I could not shut out the vision of the young people coming into Nampyeong yesterday morning. They were so full of life and accomplishment. They were the future of Korea!

After a minute or so I gazed up, my head a bit clearer. The air smelled of rich soil, young rice plants, and other unidentifiable greenery. The serenity was surreal. There was no one around and yet, it seemed as if dozens of souls haunted this place. The sun continued to warm my back, the birds chirped, and the gingko flashed their flat leaves. Who were the witnesses here? Maybe not a soul.

I got up and back on my bike and started to pedal again, still north toward Gwangju. Inner voices bombarded me. I counted my pedal revolutions again, but I couldn't drive the thoughts away.

"What's so fucking wrong with people demonstrating?" I shouted. Someone needed to pay for the massacre they'd committed. But then, despair set in. Who was going to hold Chun and his military accountable? Maybe no one.

My interaction with the *halmeoni* outside the Gwangju post office came back to me. "You must tell our story!" she'd said. She was right. The world beyond Korea had no idea what had happened. In fact, I thought, no one except the perpetrators knew what happened to the people on the bullet-penetrated buses that I had just passed. We needed witnesses.

Although it was a gentle, slightly downhill ride, I had to concentrate to keep going—right foot down, then left foot down. The warm sun and bucolic setting both did their best to soothe and calm me, and the next kilometer seemed almost peaceful. I'd not seen a single person besides the soldiers in the last hour. But, could the soldiers be considered "humans"?

Up ahead I saw that the truck remained perched on the guard box next to the railroad tracks, but its twisted carcass was no longer smoldering. Another roadblock faced me. I shuddered slightly until I noticed that this roadblock was not manned by menacing soldiers but by a hodgepodge of civilians. Their roadblock consisted of a couple of upturned two-wheeled carts normally used for carrying charcoal, considerably less sturdy than what the soldiers used. Everyone was dressed as if going to work or class—with the exception of the white sashes that a few wore.

As I drew near, every face registered surprise. I stopped and dismounted and was immediately encircled, feeling embraced rather than threatened. Questions came rapid-fire.

"Sorry, I only speak a little Korean. Please speak slowly," I said, raising my hands in an attempt to slow things down. My bike leaned against my hip and my day pack stuck to my sweat-stained shirt.

Although they understood my request, it seemed as if they were about to burst. They slowed down—a bit.

"Where are you coming from?"

"Naju."

"What's happening in Naju?"

"Nothing. It's quiet. There are no soldiers there."

"Did you ride your bike all of the way from there to here?"

"Yes."

"Did you see soldiers along the way?"

"Yes, about ten kilometers from here. There were buses and cars and …" I paused, both to compose myself and to try to find the word for "bullet holes."

One of the young men with a white sash, who was carrying a rifle over his shoulder, peered at me and my bike with a sad downturn of his mouth.

"We've been here since the early morning. You're the first person to come to Gwangju," he said.

I struggled to describe the scene of the destroyed buses. I said "there were no people" when what I meant was "there were no bodies." My voice started to crack and I gripped my bike for support while trying to talk. I felt completely drained.

"Our friends were on those buses. We've not seen them since yesterday," said another young man. His statement hushed the group, some of whom were now staring at their feet. Seconds passed without a word spoken. I glanced back up the empty road I had just traveled and wondered who the next person to come down the road would be. I feared that that person would be wearing a uniform and carrying a weapon. I longed to see the joy of yesterday in Nampyeong. That joy was gone.

There was a sense of order and organization even though the upturned carts were makeshift. I looked at the people surrounding me. Everyone was friendly, yet the scene was tense. One young man seemed to be the leader of the group wearing white sashes. If I was the only person getting in, I thought it likely that no one was getting out. Maybe some of these people were from Naju and surrounding towns, unable to leave.

Thirty minutes later, after I answered more questions about what I saw in Nampyeong yesterday and then, on my way to this spot today, I felt more optimistic than an hour before. These people were organized and committed. Maybe they didn't know what would happen in the future, but they seemed to know what they had to do now.

I walked my bike toward the wide thoroughfare that linked the center of town to the Naju road. The road was uncharacteristically free of traffic. There were only a few people milling around in a street that looked like a war zone. People seemed to be starting the process to reclaim ownership of their space in town. There were glass fragments everywhere. Two mangled green Hyundai Pony taxis sat on the side of the road. I knew if I rode my bike I'd get a flat tire. I walked.

I knocked on the gate of Tim's house and the *ajumeoni* opened it. Her eyes showed surprise and, after our greetings, she invited me in.

"No one's home. They've gone to a rally in front of the provincial building," she said.

"Can I keep my bike here?" I asked.

"Sure. Put it over there next to Ok-jin's," she said.

As I walked it over, I remembered the list of Hohyewon students. I parked my bike and went back to the gate, where she was still standing. I was relieved to see that she didn't appear as concerned as she had a couple of days ago.

"Some of the Hohyewon families have students in Gwangju. They're worried," I said as I pulled out the list from my pack and handed it over to her. "I have a favor. Could you call them to make sure they're okay?"

"Sure. I'm just going out, but I'll call when I get back," she said. I sighed with relief. "Don't worry," she added.

My thanks seemed to make her uncomfortable. I knew little about Ok-jin's mother, the *ajumeoni* in whose house Tim lived. Tiny, as all women of her generation were, this self-possessed woman was unusual in that she was divorced and her son lived with her. Her elder daughter was already married but living nearby. Tim had told me that Ok-jin had no contact with his father. She had taken Tim as a boarder to help cover her living expenses. In all of my time visiting this house my interactions with her were minimal, generally a series of thank-yous for the food she provided and a place to sleep from time to time. She must have been worried sick about her adult children during the last week. Her world had been turned upside down.

She closed the gate and headed off. I went the opposite direction, toward the center of town. The gutted buses and taxis that had littered the streets a couple of days ago were gone, but a bulldozer sat halfway in a massive hole, originally dug for an underground walkway. It reminded me of the choking tear gas in the underground walkway in Seoul.

I heard the roar of the rally before I saw it. To my ear, the microphone and amplifier seemed to chew up all of the words. The tone, however, was crystal clear—there was defiance and pride in the speakers' voices. I came up to the rally from a side street rather than the main road, still not quite sure what to make of it. A massive crowd filled the central plaza-like area around the large fountain in front of the provincial office building.

There was no way I was going to find my friends here. I gave up the search and shifted my attention to the rally itself. The young man speaking over the crackly microphone made a statement that was greeted by sustained cheers from everyone. I struggled to understand the words, hindered by the faulty microphone. My dictionary was no help. Even though I was at the outside edge of the crowd, I could see over the crowd to the speakers. They were standing on the side of the fountain. The animated crowd consisted mostly of young people, but there were many older folks cheering too.

A vision of the bullet-scarred buses between Nampyeong and the outskirts of town rose in my mind, but they seemed a million miles away from the people encircling the fountain. This was joyous defiance, suggesting that the horrors of the past week were the foundation for something important. Was this a beginning of political change in Korea?

I looked around for my friends. In the crowd of tens or hundreds of thousands, I figured that tall, blond Tim would be easy to spot, but I couldn't find him. As the young man was speaking, a ruckus erupted near the fountain. A few men frog-marched a man through the crowd to the fountain. People hurled insults and spat on him, and it appeared that if he had not been protected, the crowd would have attacked him. Around me, I heard people use the word "spy" and, as he was muscled up to the side of the fountain, a glance at his buzz-cut hair suggested that he was from the military.

Suddenly, everyone's attention was snatched by a military truck barreling toward the crowd. It screeched to a halt in the middle of the street and the driver jumped out.

"The military has invaded Gwangju! They're coming here!" he shouted.

The crowd panicked. People fled into the surrounding side streets. As we were at the edge of the crowd, two spry *halmeoni* and I ended up in front of one surge out of the plaza. The three of us rounded the corner onto another road.

"Oh, shit!" escaped my lips at the same time that the *halmeoni* shrieked. There was another military vehicle heading directly toward us. Just ten meters in front of us, a young man with a rifle crouched down into a firing position to face the oncoming threat. We tried to slow down but couldn't stop as the crowd continued to flow out of the plaza behind us. The *halmeoni* clung to each other, not sure what to do. The crowd, still moving forward, parted around us.

"They're our friends. They're not the soldiers!" a loudspeaker boomed behind us.

The message got through instantly. The tension in the crowd dissipated as if a rock had rippled a pond. The young man got up from his crouched position, propped the rifle over his shoulder, and sauntered away. People turned around and headed back toward the plaza. The *halmeoni* ambled off elsewhere, probably wondering about the wisdom of being on the streets today.

My heart beat furiously, as I tried to make sense of everything going on around me. During all of this, I'd not spoken a word to the people near me. The speed of the actions, the confusion, the excitement of the crowd, and my inadequate Korean had all conspired against me.

I turned around and headed back to the plaza. Within minutes, the low propeller beat of a small plane merged with the sound of the crowd. I paid little attention, watching people re-form around the fountain to listen to more speakers. A few minutes later, the still air filled with pepper gas— irritating but not overwhelming. Fists shook skyward as a second plane came into view discharging more pepper gas. Some people had had enough and the numbers started to thin.

I was starving. I realized that the last time I had eaten was in my home that morning. As I walked slowly back to Tim's house, I searched for a *gage* to get some food. Most shops were closed up tight, but near Tim's one stood open—a few items out front to attract clientele. Inside, a small table and a couple of chairs crowded the six-by-six-meter room with a small doorway in the back. A fridge stocked with bottles of beer and soda, a large rack of cigarettes, and bags of snacks completed the scene.

"Were you at the rally at the provincial office building?" the *ajumeoni* who ran the shop asked as she pointed toward the provincial office.

"Yes. It's still going on, but the number of people has shrunk. Do you have ramen?" I asked, my mouth watering.

"We still have ramen, but the market wasn't open today so I don't have any onions to put in it. Is that okay?" she said.

"Do you have eggs?" I asked, hopeful.

"Yes, a few," she said.

"Oh, never mind. Just ramen with some kimchi will do," I said. I didn't want to take the last of her eggs. She disappeared through the door in the back. Soon I could hear the sound of water boiling, followed by the plop of a ramen packet and the clank of metal chopsticks. The smell of kimchi brought a sense of normalcy and familiarity to the late afternoon. She placed the pot of steaming noodles in front of me and I attacked them with a set of metal chopsticks from a small tray. As my chopsticks did battle with the noodles and kimchi, I watched individuals and groups, out with brooms and buckets, start to bring order to their world. I savored every drop of the ramen broth and put down the spoon with satisfaction. I wondered if we were all in the calm eye of a massive storm.

At Tim's house, I was surprised to see Dave, a Peace Corps Volunteer from a county south of Naju. Tim said that Judi had gone back to her place on the other side of town. Each of us related what we'd seen in the last twenty-four hours. The details varied, but we all mentioned shock, anger, and "can't believe it" more than once.

Ok-jin, who had been sitting next to Tim, got up and turned on the TV. It beamed in from outside Jeonnam. The announcer berated the students and other "rabble-rousers" in Gwangju and showed footage from previous days when the military was still in control. We were stunned when the announcer said that it was footage from the events of today!

"Have you heard what they're saying about the massacre on the news?" Tim asked me.

"No, what?" I asked. I had completely forgotten that the rest of Korea might be talking about Gwangju.

"They're calling the demonstrators 'communists' and saying that they are sympathetic to North Korea," said Tim.

"What? That's bullshit!" I shouted. We seemed to career from one outrage to the next. It dawned on me that what I had seen and heard was not part of the narrative being fed to the rest of the country. What actually happened in Gwangju was being hidden.

Pictures of one of the Gwangju TV stations on fire filled the screen. The news broadcaster related that "riotous students destroyed property

A citizen militia patrolled Gwangju to prevent incursions by the military. The captured military vehicles were also used to deposit and pick up defenders at the city outskirts.

The civilian militia guarded the outskirts of Gwangju, occasionally engaging in firefights with the military.

Carbine rifles were stacked in the Jeonnam Provincial Office building. All weapons collected by the citizen militia were stored here until they were distributed to the civilian militia for defense.

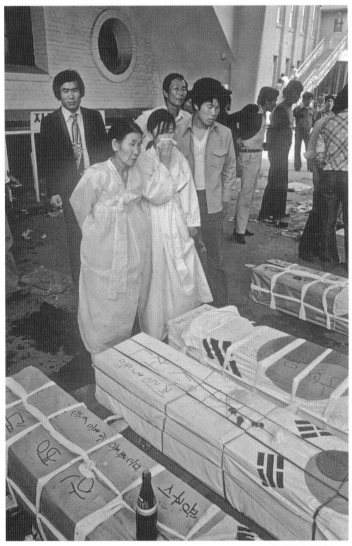

Women mourn while waiting to collect the coffin of a relative killed during the uprising

Family members of a slain citizen keep watch over his coffin

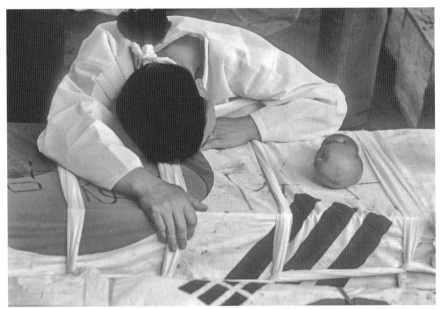

A woman wearing traditional Korean *hanbok* grieves on the coffin of a relative. A wooden Buddhist *moktak* (hollow wooden percussion instrument) rests on the coffin next to her.

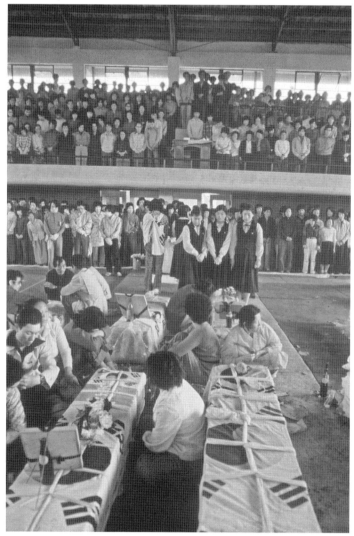

The Gymnasium Hall filled with mourners and coffins as the full extent of the massacre and uprising became apparent

A grandmother weeps over a coffin in the temporary mortuary set up next to the Jeonnam Provincial Office.

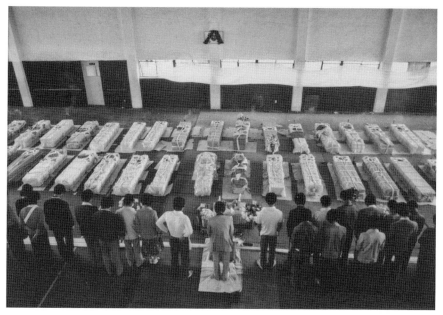

Inside the Gymnasium Hall residents look down upon the rows of coffins being readied for burial.

A coffin is loaded on a truck at the Jeonnam Provincial Office to be taken for burial.

A man carries a hastily built coffin on his bicycle.

After the military retook Gwangju in the early morning of May 27 protesters were rounded up and imprisoned.

A church service was held for schoolchildren during the final days of the uprising.

Four US Peace Corps Volunteers (Judi Chamberlin, Tim Warnberg, Paul Courtright, and Dave Dollinger) preparing for interview by German reporter, Jürgen Hinzpeter on the roof of the Jeonnam University Hospital

Paul Courtright in Hohyewon in January 1980

House in Naju where Paul Courtright lived. It was near the health centre where he worked his first six months in Korea.

Bicycle waiting for its rider

Yeontan (charcoal briquettes used for heating and cooking) stacked underneath the small porch at a house

and loyal troops are trying to keep the peace." There was no mention of atrocities committed by the soldiers. All blame was put on the students. The broadcaster went on to mention the real bogeyman: the evil influence from North Korea. I almost exploded. "What the hell? Is that what the government is saying about Sunday?"

Ok-jin, still stunned from the events of the day, concurred. "Yes, that's what they have been saying."

I just couldn't believe it. "Does *anyone*, outside of Gwangju, know what really happened?"

"No. We don't think so," Ok-jin said. "It seems that Chun wants to isolate us."

It all made sense, in an evil and manipulative way. The broadcast and reality were so vastly different. With a look of disgust on his face, Ok-jin got up and switched off the TV. The message being broadcast throughout Korea was that the uprising in Gwangju was perpetrated by a group of rebellious, destructive, communist-sympathizing young people. This was the story they wanted all Koreans outside of Jeonnam to believe.

"You saw the buildings that were burned?" asked Tim.

"Yeah..."

"Those were the two TV stations. People were so angry with the military government and Chun for how they've been portraying what happened that they set them on fire yesterday. It serves 'em right," Tim finished, anger distorting his voice.

"If Koreans in the rest of the country knew of the massacre, they, or at least the students, would be demonstrating in every city on every day," Dave said.

"If they knew that the people here had driven out Chun's army, they might try to do the same," I added.

But we listened to TV announcers in Seoul telling a story that simply was not true. The lies set off a long discussion among us.

"Hearing this, there's going to be zero support for the people of Jeonnam in the rest of the country," Tim lamented.

"Yeah, and this demonizing of the people of Jeonnam only plays into the regional stereotypes already held by many people from other provinces," added Dave.

"The military's not going to let the people of Gwangju stay in control for long. They're going to move back in and take control. It's just a matter of when," I said.

"Agreed. The question isn't 'will' the military retaliate, but 'when.' From the rally today it's clear there's little interest in giving up," Tim said, voicing the same view that we all seemed to have—both of the military and the people in Gwangju.

Tim's *ajumeoni* brought out some food, and I was relieved to have eaten earlier. I didn't want to be a burden on her food supply. While Tim and Dave ate we heard gunfire in the distance. We didn't jump. We were not used to the sound of gunfire, but it didn't shock us as before.

"The city is now surrounded and there is no food coming in," Tim said, looking at his rice. Tim didn't intend to make us feel unwelcome, but I wondered why I should stay in Gwangju. There was nothing I could do here. I excused myself and went to the cooking area to find the *ajumeoni*.

"Thank you for helping us," I said to her, unable to find more meaningful words to express myself.

"Don't mention it. This is a difficult time for everyone. We're grateful that you're all here," she responded. "I called the numbers you gave me. The students were not there, but the people who answered all said that the students are fine."

"Really?" escaped my lips without thinking. She nodded. "Many thanks," I added, unable to help myself. Koreans were uncomfortable with the American habit of saying "thanks" so easily, and I was as guilty as the rest. It was not that Koreans weren't thankful; they just showed it rather than said it.

Back in the small room, mats had been rolled out and Ok-jin, Tim, and Dave had stretched out to sleep. I undressed, took the last spot on the floor, and was out.

Day 10

Friday, May 23:

We are all "impure elements"

—

In the cool morning air, we folded up our sleeping mats and stacked them next to the wall. The *ajumeoni* had already put rice, kimchi, dried seaweed, and bean sprouts on a low lacquered table. Still stiff from sleep, I struggled to cross my legs to sit on the floor. The metal bowls containing rice were topped with metal lids, keeping the rice warm. Beside each rice bowl, a larger, but shallower, metal bowl contained seaweed soup, still giving off steam in the morning coolness. The steel chopsticks and spoon at the right side of the bowls beckoned me. The kimchi this morning was "*mul-kimchi*," a clear, spicy broth with only a few vegetables. It was the least expensive form of kimchi and another indication of the growing lack of variety of food available in town. We tucked in without a word and enjoyed the warmth of the food in front of us. Before coming to Korea I had no experience with Korean food, but I'd learned to look forward to rice and kimchi.

I felt guilty eating from the dwindling supplies in the house and in town. It was graciously offered, and I figured that the *ajumeoni* would be horrified to know that I ate less in order to ensure that they didn't run out of food. Like most Koreans I'd met, she was unfailingly polite and generous. I only ate about two-thirds of my rice although I wanted to devour it all. I made sure that the remaining rice was sparkling white—there was no residue from the other foods to contaminate it. You could mess up your own rice, but that meant you needed to eat it all. Leaving "dirty" rice was a major eating transgression that I had learned about early in my time in Korea.

Dave and I went out to see if we could learn anything new on the street. There were many unanswered questions and lots of rumors. We closed the front gate behind us.

"The TV broadcast we watched last night is really going to piss people off," I said.

Dave frowned. "Yep, but then what happens?"

"I've no idea. But there's no way the people can hold off the military circling the town."

"Yeah, I know we're supposed to remain apolitical, but that's just not possible anymore," said Dave, rubbing his forehead.

"Agreed. How do we convince Peace Corps that we're only observers? We all know how we feel. Those assholes who killed people need to be brought to justice!" I said, struggling to control my anger. But a wave of helplessness overtook me. With Chun and the military in charge, I knew that there'd be no justice. I let out a heavy sigh.

"I'm struggling to figure out what I can do. About the only thing I can think of is to talk to the media, but there are no media here," Dave said.

"Yeah, there's nothing. Except for all those lies on the TV about this," I said, gesturing at the area in front of us. "And I don't see how we can change that."

We neared the bus station and before I could continue, the sound of a small plane grabbed our attention. More pepper gas? But when we gazed up, we saw small white leaflets fluttering down. Within a minute, several kids shot out from the metal gates of the small houses on the street. Schools were closed and the kids, freed from their school uniforms, were now freed from their homes. Their faces lit up as they scampered to catch the fluttering papers. A couple of boys started a contest to see who could catch the most leaflets. They laughed as they jumped into the air, the sheets of paper dancing off their fingers. It was pure childhood joy. The absence of vehicles on the streets gave them a large playground, and within a couple of minutes more children poured out—running, jumping, laughing, calling out to their friends. Their lighthearted fun was in stark contrast to the grim reality of what was taking place in Gwangju.

The few adults out in the street did not show the same joyous abandon, although maybe, like me, they also wanted to run and jump and catch the leaflets. Dave and I chuckled as we picked up a couple of the papers. We elbowed aside two young boys who were becoming particularly proficient in their collecting. The boys backed off, but with smiles on their faces.

Dave had been in Korea a few months longer than I had. Still, we needed my dictionary to translate the message on the leaflets. They informed the people of Gwangju that the military knew the identity of the "impure elements" responsible for the uprising, and they were certainly not the good citizens of Gwangju. Rabble-rousers and North Koreans were blamed. The bottom half of the leaflet was more threatening and ominous. The immediate return of all weapons taken during the uprising was demanded. Dave and I headed back to Tim's place, the exuberance of the children forgotten.

"If they think that words like these will change people's minds, they're crazy," said Dave with disgust.

"Yeah, they're clueless as to how people think. There is no mention of an apology for the massacre that they committed!"

Like Dave, I couldn't imagine that people in Gwangju would simply roll over and acquiesce to the military. It seemed likely that the overwhelming firepower of the soldiers had silenced everyone in the smaller towns outside of Gwangju. Besides, the universities were in Gwangju, not in the smaller towns. I wondered if the military was now going house to house in the rural areas rounding up "impure elements." Had they expanded their control to include all of Jeonnam, except for the city of Gwangju?

"Do you think that Chun even knows what happened here?" Dave asked.

"He has to know about the killings. Hell, the soldiers were from his home province," I said. The fact that the military had been pushed out of Gwangju was a new twist. I wondered how Chun and his cronies would know what was happening inside the city now.

"Spies," I said, coming to a dead stop. "Spies, of course."

"What?" said Dave, as he stopped a foot ahead of me and turned around.

"Well, it just struck me. Chun must have spies here in Gwangju. Getting someone into Gwangju would probably be fairly easy, as long as they didn't use the roads. If they caught one guy, like yesterday at the rally, there are more who have not been caught," I said, shifting from one foot to the other.

"Yeah, and if there are military spies it means that pretty much any time we step outside we'll be observed. Show up at a rally? Yep, that will be observed. It'll also be recorded and reported," said Dave.

"Ah, shit," I said, frustrated. I wondered again what I was doing here. I'd been a witness. I still wanted to be a witness, but I also thought that being a witness without a voice was useless, and idiotic.

Dave and I walked on. I wondered who might be the other Western witnesses. There were some American missionaries in Gwangju. There was the guy who ran the US Information Service office. That was about it. I hadn't met the missionaries. I figured that they were probably hunkered down for the duration. I'd visited the USIS office a few times to read some newspapers or magazines but didn't really know the guy who ran the office.

"Do you have any idea what the US government's saying or doing about Gwangju?" I asked Dave.

"No idea. But I can't see Chun moving back into Gwangju without some kind of agreement from the US military."

"Yeah, you're probably right. But shit, that would make the US government complicit in the atrocities! Do you think the embassy knows what *really* happened here?" I asked with growing frustration.

"Well, if they do know, and do nothing, they're going to get an earful from me!" Dave shouted. But our anger had nowhere to go, leaving us both with a sense of impotence. What was the point of unloading on Dave, who felt the same way I did?

We arrived back at the house, picked up Tim, and walked to the site of the previous day's rally. The streets were swept of broken glass and other debris. Gwangju had started to look like its old self again. I gazed over the cleaned streets and it struck me that there was no money to pay anyone to clean. All of this work must have been done voluntarily. I wondered who had organized it.

It was early enough that most small stores were still shuttered. The plaza was up ahead, with the provincial capital building on the other side. It swarmed with people but, as we got closer, we could see that there were a series of lines leading to tables set up next to the front of the building. Hand-painted banners above the tables announced the names of various universities and other organizations. Young people sat at the tables and collected information from each person in line. A couple of lines must have included at least a hundred people and more were lining up. Registration was orderly, with people registering for a whole range of activities, including cleaning up the town. Everyone was getting down to business. People were recreating the city government, on their own terms. Some people, already signed up, went through the front gate of the provincial office building. Others emerged, with rifles across their chests or settled on their shoulders. A large white sash helped identify the emerging citizen militia.

Although I'd missed it, the rally yesterday must have included some logistical information. A request had gone out to collect weapons, with the provincial office building as the place to stockpile them. It appeared to me that in the hour or so since the leaflets had fluttered down from the sky, attitudes had hardened. Rifles were being collected, but not to turn over to the military.

Being foreigners, we started to draw a crowd. It made me feel uncomfortable. We were a distraction.

"Guys, I'm going to grab my bike and head back to Hohyewon. There's nothing meaningful I can do here," I said. Tim and Dave both stopped and stared at me.

"Okay, but do you think you can make it out?" asked Tim.

"Well, I'm not sure. If I get out I'll contact Peace Corps and let them know what's really happening here." I felt that was another good justification to leave. I struggled with conflicting emotions. There was little I could do that Tim couldn't do better, since he had better Korean and he knew the city. There was no food coming into Gwangju and I was an extra mouth to feed. But I liked the idea of being in the middle of history in the making.

"Be careful. I don't trust the soldiers," said Tim, brow furrowed.

"Yeah, I don't trust 'em either," I responded, adding as I turned to go, "You guys take care too."

I walked back the way we had come but had only managed a dozen steps when three young men materialized in front of me. They all wore spectacles, were a couple of centimeters shorter than me, and had on the typical university attire of dress shirt and slacks. I wanted to be on my way if only to get home before dark. I knew that even with my bike, it was going to be a hard slog up the hill and over to Nampyeong.

I got the sense that the students really wanted to ask me some questions, though, so I stopped. We went through the cursory polite greetings but, after that, they didn't bother with any of the "twenty questions" about me. It only took a minute before we were talking seriously.

"Did you see what the military did to our people?" one of the students asked.

"Yes, but I only saw a bit. What I saw was horrible," I said. I had heard about so much more that had transpired. Talking with Tim and others over the last few days had given me many details. Tim had said that the scale of the atrocities during the first few days in Gwangju was still being discussed. The estimates of the numbers killed ranged from around three hundred to ten times that number. There was no official tally. We'd heard claims that the military had taken away the dead so they couldn't be counted. So much had happened over such a large area. I wasn't sure how anyone could ever capture an accurate picture.

"Does the American government support Chun?" asked one student. His tone wasn't belligerent, but it was the question I'd dreaded. I wanted to crawl into a hole. He was respectful, if only because I was a few years older than him. How could I respond? Like him, I had no idea what was going on outside of Gwangju. I couldn't imagine President Jimmy Carter supporting Chun's actions. The real question the student seemed to be asking me was, "Does the American military in Seoul support Chun?"

"The American people support you," I said with a slight stammer. Hell, the American people had no idea what had happened here. Was I lying to these students? Who was I to represent America or Americans?

"Yes, but did your government allow this?"

"I don't know," was my truthful but inadequate response.

"You foreigners must tell the story. No one knows what has happened here. No one in Korea. No one outside of Korea," said one of the other students. I felt a huge weight of responsibility.

"Yes, I'll try," I said. I was deep in a hole and dirt was piling up around me. I'd been given that task already but couldn't figure out how to fulfill it. And I was sure that if I were able to get out of here and talked about what I saw, the Korean military would have me kicked out of the country. I wasn't ready to leave Korea. What was I supposed to do? I wanted to follow the guidelines laid down by the Peace Corps. *Don't get involved. Don't engage in political acts. Don't voice your opinion about local politics. Don't threaten our position as guests here in Korea.* But, given what I'd seen, how was that even possible?

The three students turned and joined one of the lines. I watched them for a few seconds and wondered if they'd be on the front line with white sashes and rifles by the end of the day. I shook slightly, imagining it. It was possible that later today, one of them might have to shoot at a fellow Korean or that he might be shot himself. Oh God, what a mess!

I was confused and frightened, but I had to get moving. I got my bike, told the *ajumeoni* my plans, and headed for the front gate. She ran after me and put two hard-boiled eggs in my hand. I protested, but she wouldn't take them back. I gently put the eggs in my pack and thanked her. I mounted my bike and planted my feet on the pedals, one down, then the other, and I was back on the street to the south edge of town. It was now clean and tidy. No broken glass, no ripped-up sidewalk tiles, no burned-out vehicles.

There was calmness to the activity of pedaling and my brain started working through a plan. I'd leave Gwangju the same way I entered the day before. I'd bike through the military roadblock at the top of the hill, ride down to Nampyeong, then take the dirt road to Hohyewon. It was fairly simple.

At the railroad tracks, the truck that was smoldering two days previously still sat atop the guard station. On the other side of the tracks, a large amorphous crowd that included a few people with rifles and white sashes stood in conversation. The upturned carts were gone. In front of the tracks, I dismounted, bumped my bicycle across, and waded through the crowd.

"Mr. Ko, Mr. Ko!" came a voice I recognized. I turned around and found diminutive Miss Kim from the Naju Health Center. She came toward me with rapid-fire questions, as if I'd miraculously become fully fluent in Korean.

"Slowly, slowly," I said to her as I smiled and pushed down the air with my hands to slow her down.

She took a breath and calmed down. As always, she was dressed immaculately, in a skirt with a blouse and tight sweater on top. Today, however, instead of her mid-high heels she wore practical trainers. We spent a few minutes getting caught up on where she'd been and where I'd been. She'd come to Gwangju a few days ago to see some relatives. She said nothing of the massacre in Gwangju and, following her lead, neither did I. She glanced toward the road to Naju.

"I heard that the military isn't allowing anyone to leave Gwangju," she said. Others around us, who'd been listening in, confirmed her statement. No one was allowed to leave Gwangju.

"Let's go," I said, surprising myself with my resolve. It seemed preposterous to me that someone could stop me from going home. Was it arrogance, ignorance, stubbornness, or some of each that led to my decision?

I watched her perplexed look change to one of determination. Without another word, Miss Kim got on the back of my bicycle. I mounted and pedaled toward Nampyeong. I could hear a lot of murmuring and talking behind us, but no one called for us to stop.

Miss Kim was light, but there was no way I was going to power both of us over the hill. After about fifteen minutes of slogging I suggested that we walk.

The road was eerily empty. Not a single person was in sight. The only sound was the rustling of the trees. Rather than feeling ominous, the silent air was calming. I felt invigorated. We were a couple of kilometers from the carnage I'd seen yesterday. Here, the road was clean. In my new habit, I examined carefully the sides of the road—there were no rifles.

We rounded the next bend and came face to face with a line of tanks and soldiers—a new roadblock. Miss Kim's gasp startled me. We both stiffened. Gaining strength and purpose from each other, we stared straight ahead. Sweat started to dampen my shirt back. We kept walking forward.

"I'm an American Peace Corps Volunteer. I live in Naju County and work at the health center!" I yelled, still about five meters away. Indicating Miss Kim at my side, I added, "Miss Kim works with me at the health center." We kept a slow, deliberate pace forward, not pausing.

I couldn't bring myself to ask permission to pass. I was scared, but I was also angry. Gripping the handlebars a little bit harder than normal, I stared into the barrel of one of the tanks. My legs trembled slightly. I alternated my gaze between the tanks and the soldiers—none had moved one inch since we first saw them. The metallic smell of the three tanks facing us and aimed at Gwangju was menacing. I found it impossible to imagine tanks rumbling down the city streets of Gwangju, but here they were. Even more inconceivable was the idea that these massive killing machines would be used against people sharing the same language, heritage, and nationality. What were the guys manning the tanks thinking? Didn't they share the same dreams and aspirations for the country as the people of Gwangju?

The peace and beauty behind the last bend in the road seemed miles away. I concentrated on every move. We stopped about two meters from the menacing line of men and machines. Miss Kim stood a little bit behind me and remained silent. I repeated my statement, emphasizing the word "American."

"You cannot pass. Go back!" barked the soldier nearest to us. He was a clone of the others gathered around the tanks, all wearing the same uniform and the same reflecting sunglasses.

"Why can't we go to Naju?" I asked, my voice hardening. I wanted to yell, "Why have you killed people in Gwangju?" but kept that question from exploding out of my mouth. The soldiers and the tanks scared the hell out of me and I knew Miss Kim must be terrified. The soldier continued to face us down. I wanted to snatch his sunglasses and grind them under my shoe.

"We have work," I continued. "I have leprosy patients who need care."

"No one is allowed to leave Gwangju by order of General Chun," Sunglasses said. His lips barely moved and he didn't budge any muscles in his compact body. His face was a blank slate. Another minute passed and no one moved. The back of my shirt was soaked. I didn't want the soldiers to see the sweat stains.

"Let's go," said Miss Kim, pulling at my shirt. I reluctantly turned to observe her. She could probably read the situation better than I. I gave her a slight grim nod, turned back to the soldiers for one final glare, and took in a huge breath. The acrid smell of the tank was almost overpowering.

The soldiers continued to stand rooted to the spot. We could've been a pair of pesky flies as far as they were concerned. No one was allowed to pass and the fact that I was an American didn't change that. I wondered, though, if being a foreigner was keeping them from shooting us. I was sure that they would report back that a "round eye" was in Gwangju.

I struggled to understand these guys. They were about my age, maybe a couple of years younger. Up until a week ago, my view of Korean soldiers was fairly simple. All Korean men had to serve in the military, and the male university students I was friends with included those who'd already put in their military time and those who were going to do so in the next year or so. They were decent guys, normal guys. Sunglasses and his colleagues seemed different. Rumors swirled around Gwangju that the soldiers had been drugged to encourage them to attack. We'd heard that they'd been told that communists had infiltrated Gwangju. What else had happened to enable them to kill fellow countrymen? With their sunglasses it was impossible to see their eyes—which increased my disgust and helplessness.

We turned around and started the trudge back to Gwangju, my damp shirt visible for all to see. I wanted to jump on my bike and pedal like hell to get away from the soldiers, but pride prevented me from such a recognizable retreat. I shuddered at the thought of the tank and rifle barrels pointed at our backs. Our heads were up until we passed out of sight of the soldiers. Around the bend, Miss Kim and I walked on with heads down. After a few minutes, Miss Kim lifted her head.

"I'm afraid. What's going to happen next?" she asked.

"I don't know. I don't trust Chun. And I sure as hell don't trust those soldiers," I said, jerking my head back in the direction from which we had just come.

"Why do they have tanks facing us? We are all Korean!" Miss Kim said, her brow creased.

The tanks also bothered me. How did they plan on using them? If the goal was to create fear, it worked. They certainly had me scared.

"I heard that they think 'the North' is behind the uprising," I said.

"That's false. And they know better," she said, a sharp edge to her voice.

"Yeah. Maybe they're searching for excuses to justify their actions," I answered. The soldier had mentioned "General Chun." Just hearing that name made me mad. I didn't believe he and his senior officers cared about the people and I didn't think this was going to end well.

We approached the crowd at the railroad tracks. I saw people point toward us and all faces turned in our direction. Before we had started, I had wondered if some of the people would be curious to see if the "round eye" could get out. Although they talked with each other, I couldn't hear them yet. As we got closer, the ripple of conversation stopped.

I put my head down, ashamed of my failure. I didn't want to try to explain. I wanted only to keep track of where each foot landed as I plodded ahead. I felt useless, frustrated, and humiliated.

The crowd parted for me and my bike. Miss Kim hung back. She was cocooned and the group of people peppered her with questions. There was nothing I could say that she couldn't say better. Nothing. I kept walking.

At Tim's, my head still hung low as I handed the boiled eggs back to the *ajumeoni*. I walked in, and Tim, Dave, and Judi glanced up in surprise. I was equally surprised to see Judi back. A couple of days ago she'd said that her plans were to just "hunker down" with her Korean family across town. Something must have changed.

I sat on the floor next to Tim and my shoulders sagged as I related the story of the roadblock.

"That's not a good sign," said Tim.

"I felt completely useless today. There's nothing we can do. The military's not going to let this end well. They're a bunch of arrogant assholes!" I shouted, finally releasing my pent-up anger. There were nods from everyone in the room.

"Yeah, that's for sure. If they're not letting us out, they're trying to isolate all of us," said Tim. Then, pointing at me, he continued, "If you couldn't get out going south, then the same is true everywhere."

"The military's going to invade soon," suggested Dave.

"They must have a tight band around the entire city. What's happened here, and is still happening here, is completely unknown outside of Jeonnam," I said, my voice still an octave higher than normal and laced with frustration.

"Things may have changed. Dave and I ran into two German TV reporters today. Somehow, information has gotten out; otherwise, those reporters wouldn't be here," countered Tim.

I sat up straight. Was there some hope after all?

"Yep, now maybe the story can get out," said Dave.

"That's the best news I've had all week!" I said.

"How'd they get into Gwangju?" asked Judi.

"They said that they came in using one of the small back roads," explained Dave. "They don't speak Korean and they have no escort. It's a wonder they made it."

"Getting in may be easier than getting out," I said as I pictured the line of tanks I'd faced a few hours earlier.

"We agreed to meet with them at eight tonight. They want to get our stories. They also want us to help translate for them," said Tim.

"Translating for reporters? Would that be okay? Would that get us into trouble?" asked Judi.

"Tim and I have been talking about that," said Dave.

"Translating means that we're not taking one side or another. We're only helping the reporters understand what people are saying," said Tim.

"Okay, so we're not giving our opinions. We're not going to be quoted, right?" I asked.

"Yep, we'll just translate what the reporters ask and what the people say," said Tim.

"But won't Chun and the military find out? I'm sure there are spies around town. If they learn that we translated for the reporters we'll be in deep shit," I said.

"Chun can rot in hell!" Dave said. We all nodded—that being the sentiment we all shared. "The Germans want to interview Tim at his hospital tomorrow," he added.

"That's great. Tim's the only one of us who can tell them about Sunday. Between translating and Tim telling what he saw, the story will get out," said Judi.

"I said that I'd tell them what I saw on Sunday but that I'd want my identity hidden. They could call me a 'foreigner in Gwangju,'" said Tim.

"Really? Don't you think that Chun will figure out it was you?" I asked. "There's only a handful of us here in Gwangju."

"Well, I think it's a risk we have to take. There are a few missionaries here, but I don't think they'll translate for the reporters. If we don't help, who will?" said Tim. I could not argue with the logic.

"Guys, there's another wrinkle we have to discuss. I had a phone call from the guy who runs the USIS here. He told me that he had a radio message from the embassy and that we've been ordered to leave Gwangju," said Judi.

"What? How?" Dave, Tim, and I responded, almost in unison.

"He said we're to go to the air base just outside of town. And that if we come upon a roadblock, we're to say that we're from the US Embassy and that we've been instructed to go to the base. We are to wait there until…" Judi faltered, her shoulders collapsed a bit, and she sighed.

"Until what?" asked Dave, probably not really expecting an answer.

"What did you tell him?" asked Tim.

"I told him that I'd talk to you. He said that we had to leave by midday tomorrow."

"Does he know who's here?" I asked, waving my hand to include Dave and me.

"I don't think so. He only mentioned Julie, Tim, and me," she said. Judi's mention of Julie, another volunteer living in Gwangju, had me wondering where she was. She must have stayed at home.

I breathed a sigh of relief. It was odd to feel relief that a member of the US diplomatic corps didn't know I was here. But then, just because he didn't list my name didn't mean I was free from the order to leave.

"He said that he's going to call back tomorrow morning," said Judi. "I thought about this on the way over and I think we should have a joint response."

"Yeah, that makes sense," Tim agreed.

"He said we can get out through the air base? But Paul couldn't get out through Naju. I don't like it. I can't leave," said Tim.

"I'm not leaving Gwangju," said Dave.

"Same for me," added Judi.

"Yeah, well, I tried once and it didn't work. I'm staying," I said. I gazed around the room. Ok-jin and his mother patiently waited for us to tell them what we were discussing. Tim briefly told them what we'd decided. When he finished, they appeared relieved.

"You know, I think we have an obligation to stay. It's an obligation to our friends here. To the people we work with here. We can't run away," said Tim.

"If we all leave, everyone in Gwangju will know it. I haven't seen any other foreigners on the street," said Judi.

"Yeah, it would send the wrong message. People would think that we gave up on them," said Tim.

"Everyone here has really taken good care of us. They don't want anything to happen to us. They're protecting us," I said.

"Given everything we've seen, the only people we should be afraid of are the soldiers," said Tim.

"Yeah, trying to cross the military lines makes no sense," I said.

"They must have no idea what's really happening here," said Dave, his arms resting on his crossed legs.

"They're not *asking* us to leave. They're *ordering* us to leave," said Judi, bringing us back to the issue facing us.

"And if we refuse? We just agreed that we're not going to leave," I said, frustrated.

"Do you think we'll be kicked out of the country?" Judi asked.

"Who knows what Chun and the military will do? The first question is, will Peace Corps and the embassy believe us? Will they back us up?" I asked.

"Well, it might depend upon what the USIS guy says when he gets to Seoul," Tim suggested.

"He's going to be pissed off if we refuse the order to leave," said Dave.

"Damn! I wish I'd gotten out today. We've got to let the embassy and Peace Corps know what's going on here," I said. I shook my head at the thought that I should have argued with Sunglasses more. I should've pushed him harder.

"Yeah, bummer. But, we're all here now. At least now we have a plan," Tim added.

The notion of being a witness had seemed fairly straightforward a few days ago. Now it had become much more complicated—and dangerous. It seemed as if the people in Gwangju had been cut adrift by their own government. In just a few days they'd gone from being part of the "we" to being the enemy. As they became the enemy, the middle ground we tried to occupy shrunk. The people in Gwangju wanted us as witnesses. The military didn't. It seemed that now, simply by being witnesses we had crossed some invisible line. There was no doubt what Chun and his coup leaders would say—they would want us out. What would our own government say? Would they back us up? Would we be allowed to stay?

I looked around at the faces in the room. Ok-jin and his mother looked as lost as we were. The big difference was, Gwangju was their home.

⟋   ⟋   ⟋

Without more to say, we divided up. I found a quiet corner and started to write. I was finding it difficult to keep track of everything going on. I'd start a sentence, then stop. I'd go back to something I'd written before. I wrote in the margins, my handwriting getting more and more cramped as the blank space on the paper continued to shrink. I sat back, wondering for whom I was writing. I sure wasn't going to describe everything I saw to Mom and Dad. I liked to write, to describe what I saw and what it might mean. I was less adept at writing how I felt, except when I was frustrated and angry. When work was busy and meaningful, I often forgot to write. Writing was now an essential activity.

A few hours later, the four of us closed the gate behind us and started to walk to the small hotel where the German reporters stayed. Along the way, we made some decisions.

"We're all staying, right? We're all ready to translate," said Tim, looking from one person to another.

"Yeah, but you're going to end up with the lion's share," I said.

"That's fine," continued Tim, with a shrug. "We'll each tell the journalists what we saw."

"We're only going to talk about what we saw. Not what we heard," said Judi, as she stared straight ahead, her jaw firm.

"Agreed. There are way too many rumors floating out there," I said.

"We're going to avoid giving any TV interviews. We'll only do TV interviews if our identity can be masked," said Tim. Three heads nodded in agreement.

The streets were still clean. It was now dark. Up ahead we could see a line of vehicles in front of the provincial office building ready for assignment. Even at this late hour, there were still some young people around. I suspected that they were either getting ready to head to the perimeter of Gwangju or had just come back from there. There was serious work to be done. The teahouses were shuttered and the drinking places empty of business. The silence of the street was eerie.

"Hey guys, we're drawing too much attention," Dave said as we neared the provincial office building. He was right. The four of us walking together was attracting a lot of looks.

"Paul and I will take this street and meet you at the hotel," said Judi as she pointed to the small street off to our right. Without another word, Judi and I peeled off and Tim and Dave continued ahead.

Tim and Dave arrived just before us. We gathered in the small hotel restaurant, sitting around a table while the reporters started taking notes. Tim's experience was the most horrific and he was the first to talk. There were no interruptions and the Germans wrote furiously. Dave, Judi, and I were rapt listeners yet again, as Tim described the episode on May 18. He'd pulled bloodied students away from soldiers. He'd intervened to prevent further beatings and possibly, death, and he'd helped carry people to the hospital. We all knew that it was the most important story to get out. At the end, he said that being tall and blond helped.

One after another, Dave, Judi, and I told our stories. As I listened to the others, I realized that although we'd all seen different things, we'd all come away with a common perspective on the wrongs committed in Gwangju. When we finished our stories, I was exhausted and it seemed that everyone else, including the Germans, were equally fatigued.

We agreed to meet them the following morning to help translate. Tim suggested a schedule. First, we'd visit the provincial office, then the mortuary that had been set up across from there, and then the hospitals. For the first time, I felt that I had a purpose being in Gwangju. We were going to be busy.

We stepped out of the small hotel. It was after ten and the streets were completely empty.

"Damn, it's past curfew," Dave said.

"We'd better stay together," Tim said. For once we wanted to stand out. We came around the front of the provincial office from one of the side streets. It was unnerving—both dark and quiet—and we all felt anxious.

"Could someone escort us back to our house?" Tim asked a couple of the young students serving as guards in front of the provincial office building.

"No, it's not safe. You should go back," came the response. It was pitch dark and there were only a few lights on. What made it "not safe"? Dave started to argue, but Tim cut him off.

"Arguing with these guys makes no sense. They're floundering, just like us. They're proud to be here. They feel responsible. They're defending their city," he said.

"Yeah, they're probably just as scared as we are. We'd better to go back to the hotel," said Judi. We turned around.

"Does anyone have any money for the hotel?" I asked as we walked. A sequence of "no" and "nope" made it clear—no one had money.

"We're going to have to ask the *ajumeoni* who runs the place if we can pay later," said Judi.

"Or we can ask the Germans if they could pay for us," I suggested.

A few minutes later, we walked up the few steps into the hotel to find two other foreigners standing in the restaurant with the Germans. We all did introductions and without a moment's hesitation, the two new foreigners said that they'd pay for our rooms.

It was nearing eleven, but Terry Anderson, an AP reporter, and Robin Moyer, a photographer for *Time* magazine, asked for a quick briefing. We were all exhausted, but we also felt that the influx of foreign reporters had upended our sense of frustration and impotence. These were the people who could get the story out. None of us begrudged doing the briefing again. So, we talked and they listened.

With the briefing done and plans reconfirmed for the next day, the *ajumeoni* handed me the key to the room for the guys and Judi headed off to her room.

We staggered down the hallway, and I opened the door and had a shock. There was a shower! After months of sponge baths or a once-a-week visit to a bathhouse, a bathroom with a shower was a luxury. Along with restaurants and teahouses, bathhouses in Gwangju were shuttered. I couldn't remember the last time I'd had a shower. After quickly undressing I stood under the hot water. The shower was a small piece of heaven. We took turns in the shower and rolled out the sleeping mats. Sleep came quickly.

Day 11

—

The tables and banners, now hanging forlornly, remained in front of the provincial office building, but no lines of people led to them. Instead, people clustered around the building's front gate. I could see that inside the provincial building compound there was a beehive of activity to organize cleanup, vehicle and weapons allocation, and all of the other logistics that required sorting out. There was no physical infrastructure to rebuild, but a system of "government" was being constructed. Gwangju was working again, as well as possible, given that the city was surrounded by hostile forces and cut off from the rest of the country. Getting things "working again" included figuring out all of the basics—food, ammunition, and saving lives.

We approached the building. Eight foreigners walking together didn't go unnoticed. There were plenty of stares from the two hundred or so people who milled around. Why were there so many people?

We had agreed to translate for the reporters, but what did translation really entail and who was to translate for whom? As we reached the office building the four of us PCVs glanced at each other, unsure of the way forward.

"We want to go inside the provincial office to meet with the leaders," said one of the German reporters. We looked at him, then at each other.

"Okay," said Tim, without much enthusiasm. I had anticipated that we would translate interviews with people on the street or those who had witnessed the massacre. I hadn't anticipated going inside the provincial office building. It struck me that translating for the "rebel leaders" would only give Chun and his cronies another excuse to get rid of us. I glanced around, wondering if Chun's spies were circulating in the crowd. I turned back to find that my friends had handed over their Peace Corps ID cards to the young, fresh-faced guards. I did the same. Tim introduced the reporters and explained our purpose. The guards' eyes lit up and they welcomed us in.

We stepped through the front gate to the wail of an approaching ambulance. A side gate opened and the ambulance entered.

"Paul, would you stay with me? I want to see what's going on with the ambulance," Robin asked. One of the German reporters nodded that he too wanted to join us.

"Okay," I said, somewhat nervous and unsure of what to make of the arriving ambulance. The rest of the team went inside.

Two young men got out of the front and opened the back of the ambulance. They reached in and pulled out a gurney with slow, deliberate movements. They stared at the body on the gurney with sadness and I didn't want to interrupt them. The two men, and the dead body of the young man on the stretcher that they placed gently on the ground, were probably two to three years younger than me. None of them could have weighed over sixty kilograms. All three wore a white sash, but the one on the body on the gurney was rumpled and bloody. Blood had also dried on his shirt where a bullet had pierced his abdomen. It was hard to look—and it was hard not to look.

"Could you ask about the young man—his name, where he was killed?" Robin asked, bringing me back to my job.

I asked the ambulance driver, my voice low and soft. I had trouble understanding his response. The driver was distraught and his voice was emotion-laden. The story gradually unfolded as he calmed down. They were three friends from the university.

"The three of us were part of a group of ten guarding the road to Hwasun. Around three in the morning, a group of soldiers tried to invade Gwangju. There was a lot of shooting, and that was when Jun-shik was shot."

"Did the soldiers get into Gwangju?" asked the German reporter.

Both the driver and his friend shook their heads "no."

"Where is Jun-shik from?" Robin asked.

"He's from Gwangju." I gestured at the two shaken young men. "He and his friends attend Jeonnam University."

"How will his family know what happened?" the German asked. As I translated, I heard shuffling to the side, and a middle-aged man came forward and took over the conversation.

"We'll notify his relatives. We'll clean him. He'll be put in an open coffin. Then he'll be put in the mortuary here," he said. I searched my dictionary— learning the words for "coffin" and "mortuary."

The ambulance driver and his companion, rings of exhaustion and pain around their eyes, asked to leave. With a nod from Robin, they picked up their guns and signed them back in just outside the provincial office. I watched them, their heads down, as they whispered with each other, and then slowly shuffled away. My heart ached and I realized I'd quit breathing. I took a gulp of air.

My attention was drawn to the people milling around the front gate. The composition of people had changed since yesterday. Today, there were as many older people as there were university students. Most of the older people were *halmeoni*. They waited, patiently and solemnly, to go into the mortuary. A gate opened and, a few at a time, they walked to the low building that the guard had indicated. There, they waited to file through the mortuary to search for loved ones—sons, daughters, grandsons, and granddaughters—who had not returned home.

"Let's go," said Robin, as he gestured toward the mortuary.

We joined a middle-aged couple and a *halmeoni* walking with slow, agonized steps. I was relieved that Robin didn't ask me to ask them any questions. How could I ask "why are you here?" Following them through the door into the makeshift mortuary it became obvious that this room, normally used for other activities, had been repurposed. Chairs and tables were stacked along the sides and, in the middle, rows of half-open pine boxes lay from one end to the other. I heard cries and I didn't want to continue.

"We need to do this. Their stories need to be told," said the German reporter, his voice just above a whisper. He was right. I had to do my part and help get the story out. The story was here, in this cavernous dimly lit hall. A shiver swept through me. Morning sunlight filtered through the windows on one side, casting light and shadow on the nearest row of pine boxes. The air-conditioning was set to full blast, chilling the air.

An earnest young man, dressed in the white coat that doctors or medical students usually wear, came over and met us. He introduced himself as a final-year medical student and said he had volunteered to help set up the mortuary. He spoke clearly and precisely and I understood him easily.

"We keep the bodies here for a short time—mainly to get them identified," he said.

"There are more bodies?" Robin asked, perplexed.

"Oh yes, most are at one of the hospitals," he said.

"How long do they stay here?" asked Robin.

"Usually just a few hours when…" The remainder of his answer was blotted out by a piercing wail. Just ahead, over his shoulder, the *halmeoni* was doubled over a pine box, her simple *hanbok* rumpled. Other people, maybe family members or maybe strangers, came to her side to give comfort. Her wailing gradually lessened and was replaced by heaving sobs. People remained by her side. I was frozen in my tracks and relieved that my colleagues respected her grief and took no pictures.

I regarded our young assistant. His face was drawn. He shuddered slightly, then led us down the rows of boxes. The massacre was almost a week ago, but there were still people dying. The image of the buses and taxis lying askew on the road to Nampyeong resurfaced in my brain. I was starting to obsess over the question of where the bodies from the bullet-pocked buses had gone.

It seemed important to me to count the number of bodies. I counted boxes, content to deceive myself, even though I knew boxes and bodies were one and the same. There were about fifty boxes. Robin stopped at a box just ahead of me.

"How was this old woman killed?" he asked. No one hovered over the pine box, so I turned to the young man in the white coat and asked him.

"She was killed when the soldiers opened fire from a helicopter. No one has identified her yet—we don't know anything about her except where she was killed," he said.

She appeared to be resting quietly. She could have been the *halmeoni* that grabbed my arm in front of the post office earlier in the week. I suspected that this *halmeoni*, if she were alive, would have made the same demand of me—bear witness and tell the story. Just as we, foreigners, often all appeared alike to Koreans, *halmeoni* all appeared alike to me. They were bent over from decades of work and carrying children and grandchildren on their backs. Their hair was always thin on top from aging and the years of carrying everything on their heads. The lines on their faces spoke of lives led, difficulties faced, and joys encountered. *Halmeoni* never relaxed; their work was never done. *Halabeoji*, grandfathers, seemed to have lives of leisure in comparison.

What kind of government would kill a *halmeoni*? How many more *halmeoni* were out there waiting to be identified, cried over, taken home, and buried? Robin walked up to small coffin next to the *halmeoni's*. Before he could ask any questions, the young assistant started.

"This child was killed at the same time. We're trying to find the mother. We're not sure if the *halmeoni* and child are related or not," he said. The body was wrapped up, except for the boy's face. We all stood there in shocked silence as if the lack of sound could bring the child back to life. After a minute, we exhaled and moved on. There was more.

No pictures were taken of the child or the *halmeoni*. Robin and the German reporter took pictures showing the scale of the place or of those grieving, rather than of the individuals resting unnaturally in pine boxes. Many of the coffins in the overpowering room held people in their late teens and early twenties. They were the future of the Korean nation and society. We walked down the last aisle. The images did not change—one life after another, linked by the simple desire to have a voice in their own destiny. These people would never tell their stories. I cast a glance at the young man in his white coat. How could he and the other young people who manned this place keep their sanity? The smells, the sounds, and the sights in the mortuary overwhelmed me. Our assistant remained polite and attentive and as we reached the front again, he waved a hand over the open space.

"You're the first foreign reporters here. Please show the world what happened." Without translating, I nodded assent. Robin, the German, and I regarded each other. I felt confident that they both clearly understood the task before them.

As we headed toward the provincial office, Robin said, "Let's get inside. I don't want to miss an interview with the leaders of the uprising." The reporters tucked away their notebooks and cameras and we walked to the front door.

The imposing, but not ostentatious, provincial office was, in fact, only a three-story building, constructed during the Japanese occupation. Its architecture matched that of most provincial office buildings and train stations throughout the country. A central staircase just inside the front door split to the right and left. There were no elevators. We found my friends and the other reporters in a large meeting room. They sat near the door, all of them leaning forward, glued to the proceedings. We joined them and I, emotionally drained, sank gratefully onto the hard seat.

A citizen committee was seated around a large oblong table. The conversation was rapid and I leaned over to Judi to get some details. The citizens around the table, some listening and others talking animatedly, numbered about eight and included the vice mayor. I didn't ask, but I wondered if the mayor had decided not to join the uprising. There were a couple of university students on the committee. They were the most animated and demanded that resistance to the military continue. They had three demands, which one youth counted out on his fingers: the release of Kim Dae-jung, the end of martial law, and the resignation of Chun Doo-hwan. There was dissension in the committee, judging by the crossed arms and firmly clenched jaws. The older men were dressed like typical businessmen with coats and ties. They wanted Gwangju to return to normal. The rest of the citizen committee, with one notable exception, wanted the same. Without saying it, it was clear that they didn't believe any of the three demands would be accepted by Chun and the military.

An elderly man seated next to the two students, stood out. He had a small white goatee—unusual, as facial hair is very uncommon in Korean men. He was dressed like an Oxford professor, with a tweed jacket and starched blue shirt underneath. Unlike the vice mayor and businessmen, he supported the student demands. Everyone around the table deferred to him; his aristocratic standing was unquestionable. Tim leaned over and told us that he'd been a freedom fighter during the Japanese occupation of Korea. No one else in the room seemed to have his gravitas. All eyes were fixed on him. "We must support our students. If we don't, the deaths in our city will have been in vain," he said in a crisp, professional manner.

"The government will never agree to the demands," responded the vice mayor, as he bowed his head in respect.

"You're right," the elderly man responded. "But we must show everyone that we are strong—and that we demand democracy."

"The military will come back into Gwangju," asserted one of the businessmen, "and more people will be killed if we resist."

"We have to show our resistance, but we'll also have to give way. We'll have to melt back into civilians," countered Mr. Goatee. One item had full agreement from everyone in the room: it was not acceptable to have the same military unit that perpetrated the massacre on May 18 enter Gwangju again.

The meeting broke up and the journalists asked to get interviews. The students left first, their faces etched in frustration. They and Mr. Goatee got out before we could request an interview. Most of the older participants didn't want to be interviewed. A couple of short interviews were arranged with a few ancillary people. One person interviewed said that one of the students on the committee didn't really represent the students. We all felt more confused than when we had arrived. Now it was the reporters who were frustrated. There appeared to be two main factions: One faction sought to get Gwangju up and running again and to find a way to negotiate with the military to remove the blockade. The other faction sought to continue resistance to the military—principally to not allow the military to enter Gwangju again. Neither faction held sway and so, both factions were exasperated.

"Let's go to the hospital," said Terry, rubbing his chin with his hand.

"We should be able to get some stories and photos there," said Robin.

"We also need to get your story, Tim," added one of the Germans, pointing toward him.

We all got up from the uncomfortable chairs. A few people rubbed their legs before we walked down the empty staircase, out into the small courtyard, and through the front gate. There were still a lot of people around the building and I felt as if I had a target painted on my back. I imagined that a spy in the crowd was going to report back that there were four young Americans who spoke Korean translating for the reporters.

Jeonnam University Hospital, where Tim worked, was set back from the street, and gingko and other trees lined the sidewalk out front. The trees provided welcome shade to those who wanted peace and rest before entering. Although not imposing, the hospital was considered the best public hospital in the province. Today the sidewalk and entry gate were crowded. There were as many people here as in front of the provincial office. We walked inside and immediately climbed the stairs to the roof, where the Germans were going to tape an interview with Tim.

After they set up, Dave and I went back downstairs. Dave and Terry took one hallway and Robin and I moved down another. We were in search of the main surgical wards to do interviews. In every narrow hallway the injured occupied the floor space. Although in neat lines against the walls, there were too many to count. The wards were already over capacity with casualties and empty beds were nonexistent. Each hallway looked just like the last. The smells assaulted me—antiseptic mixed with sorrow and death. In the wards, family members, talking quietly, sat on the floor next to their wounded sons and daughters, some in beds, others on the floor between the beds. These people had survived and their families were grateful.

In the confusion of the place, I had to ask twice where the main male and female wards were. Even then, I made a couple of wrong turns. Robin didn't seem to notice, since he managed to conduct interviews with the same people I asked directions from. The stories followed a pattern: About a week ago people marched peacefully down the street; then the soldiers, lined up at the end of a block, attacked without warning. People were shot, people were beaten, and people were bayoneted. Young people, in particular, were singled out. It seemed to me that the stories all ran together into one.

We ventured deeper into the hospital and I wondered if the situation there would be different. My thoughts were interrupted by a piercing cry. Robin and I froze. The cry came from ahead, in a room to our right. I knocked, then opened the door with slow movements, afraid what might be inside. We stepped in and closed the door quietly. There were a number of beds in the room, but most people sat or were lying on the floor. Our attention was drawn to a young man bent over a bed that cradled a young girl. She looked to be about twelve or thirteen years of age. Her face was visible, but the rest of her body was wrapped up—she was not moving. The young man cried—his voice held a mix of pain, anger, and rage. We stood there, shadows against the wall. He was oblivious to the people around him and, after a couple of minutes, two young medical students gently reached down to help him stand up and walked him out the door. A middle-aged man sitting on the floor in the room bade us over.

"The girl was his younger sister. She was brought here a few days ago. She had surgery, but…," he inhaled and continued, "she died this morning, just before her older brother arrived."

I peered closely at the middle-aged man. He was dressed in a clean but tattered shirt and pants and he had placed his shoes on a piece of cardboard to keep the floor clean. He was sitting cross-legged on the floor next to a sleeping young man with a bandage on his left leg. Pain distorted the man's face. I sat down on the floor in front of him, also cross-legged.

"How was she killed?" I asked.

"I don't know." He pointed at the young man who rested on the floor. "But like my son here, she was probably shot by the soldiers when they fired on bus and taxi drivers." He took another breath before continuing, with a small tremor. "The drivers were shielding people, trying to stop the killing."

I glanced away for a few seconds, uncomfortable and scared. My hands felt out of place, like they were trying to protect me from an unseen threat. Looking at the man, I realized that I'd not done a proper introduction and greeting and I needed to correct this. He was at least twenty years older than I was. I used the respectful form of greeting to introduce myself and Robin. My legs started to ache, but I stayed put as this man had my full attention.

"We are sorry your son was injured. Will he be okay?" I asked.

The older man, before responding, also introduced himself. He was Park Moon-chun and he lived in Damyang, north of Gwangju. I made the assumption that the young man was his only son, as he didn't refer to him as a "first son" or a "second son." I pictured their family and the sacrifice that he and his wife had made up to this point to ensure he got a good education. His son was their future. He started to fill in the details while his son continued to sleep.

"My son is a student at Jeonnam University. He's a good boy and wasn't part of the demos," he said with pride in his voice.

"How was he shot?" I asked, aware that I asked this question over and over again.

"I asked my son the same question. He said that he was with some friends when the military attacked some taxi drivers and bus drivers. You heard about this?" he asked. The room was quiet even though other groups sat in the room. Some listened to our conversation, but most tended to their sons and daughters. Cross-legged on the floor, Mr. Park had barely moved an inch from the time our conversation started.

"Yes, I heard about that from my friends," I answered, adding almost in a whisper, "I also saw buses and taxis with many bullet holes."

"What's happening to our country? Why are they doing this to us? We don't like Chun, but we were willing to let him be the president as long as we were safe and our country prospered," he said as his head sank down. With a sigh and slight heave of his shoulders, he added, "We can't go back, but we don't know how to go forward."

"I understand." My words sounded inadequate and pathetic. After translating his last statement for Robin, I added, "Thank you, uncle." I tilted my head toward Robin. "I hope my friend here can let everyone know what happened."

I uncrossed my stiff legs with difficulty, stood up and said goodbye, and wondered what was ahead for Mr. Park and his son. His calm and determined manner, even in pain, suggested to me that he wasn't going to let what happened to his son be forgotten. We turned to leave.

When we returned to the front of the hospital, the rest of our team was already there. They stood apart, slouched, drained of energy.

"I'm going home," Judi said, as we went out the front gate. "There's nothing more I can do. I'll be home until it's over." The word "over" seemed to chill the air. After brief goodbyes, she slowly strolled west.

We walked unhurriedly back to the provincial building and climbed the staircase to the meeting room where the citizen committee had reconvened. We stepped inside, took our seats on the unforgiving chairs, and tried to follow the conversation. It seemed to me that little progress had been made to reach a common approach.

I leaned over to whisper to Tim as I tried to get comfortable in the hard chair. "Men are running this committee—there's not a single woman in the room," I said.

"Huh, you're right," he said as he glanced around the room.

"I'd imagine that an *ajumeoni* could whip these guys into shape."

"Yeah, Ok-jin's mom would do a great job. She'd make sure that they reached a decision and stuck with it."

"There are a few women on the perimeter defending the town, alongside the men. They're in the hospitals. At the same time, they're the ones doing all of the cooking to help feed people here at the provincial building," said Dave, on the other side of Tim.

The citizen committee remained deadlocked. The stumbling block was: how should the people of Gwangju interact with the military surrounding the town?

"The military has a ring of soldiers and tanks all around the town. They're not interested in talking with us," said the vice mayor, reiterating a point from the morning.

"They *will* invade Gwangju. We have to decide what our response will be. People need to know," said an older businessman.

"We'll stay in the provincial building and fight the military!" the two students argued, firm in their conviction. But their main supporter, the elderly freedom fighter, had left and the students had lost some of their clout.

"If you do, you'll be killed," the vice mayor said, his voice rising. His words stilled the room. Members of the committee looked down, looked at a blank wall, looked at a pen—but not at each other. Within a minute, conversation started up again, shifting to less controversial topics.

"Tomorrow we should hold a service for the people who have died," the vice mayor said. The students slumped back into their chairs.

"Yes, good idea," another member of the committee agreed. "We'll hold another rally this afternoon. People are not ready to give up."

"Some of our friends are going to burn an effigy of Chun Doo-hwan," one of the students said. I dug in my pack for my dictionary, but Tim stopped me. He knew the Korean for "effigy." I figured that even after ten years of life and work in Korea, I still wouldn't have learned the Korean word for "effigy."

The reporters pulled their chairs together and had their own short discussion. Terry turned to us.

"We have an idea. Could you translate?" he asked. He turned to the committee.

"Excuse me for interrupting," he said, and the room became quiet. As Terry spoke, Tim translated and gestured toward Terry and the others.

"The reporters think, we think, that it would be good to hold a press conference. The world doesn't know what happened here," said Tim, his hands out, as if he could take in the entire town. "We would be happy to help you organize it."

There were nods of agreement, and I felt that the ground had just moved under our feet. A press conference would provide legitimacy to the citizen committee. It would show that the people in Gwangju were organized.

"Thank you. That's a good idea. Let's schedule it for tomorrow afternoon," said the vice mayor. Whispered conversations ran through the committee members. The vice mayor had taken the lead and it seemed that everyone on the committee was in agreement. I turned to Tim.

"Wow, a press conference? That'll give a perspective that Chun and his cronies don't want to get out. It could break this wide open," I said.

"Yeah, but the targets already plastered on their backs will get easier to see," Tim responded, as he gestured toward the committee.

"Getting a tape out of town, and out of Korea, will be no small feat," Dave added.

The meeting broke up. The outstanding issue of how to deal with the military that encircled the town remained unanswered. Views had not changed. It seemed to me that they might even have hardened.

And, in the back of my mind, another issue bothered me—the food supply continued to dwindle.

Tim walked home. The rest of us gathered back at the small restaurant at the hotel and the journalists discussed the plan going forward. After some discussion, we agreed to split up again. I would take Robin to the rally to get images from the burning of the Chun effigy. I didn't question the assignment. I felt that, for once, I had something to do. We were out the door within a few minutes.

I knew I couldn't just hang back at the edge of the crowd and watch since I now had a task. With little thought, I plowed through the crowd, with

Robin in tow. We were in search of the effigy.

"I'm sorry..." "Excuse me..." escaped my mouth every couple of minutes as I tapped people on the shoulder from behind in order to get through. Each time, the head attached to the shoulders turned around and eyes widened in surprise. I then repeated the same few words, adding an introduction of Robin, the foreign reporter. The large camera hanging from his neck drew as much attention as being a "round eye." Expansive openness and gratitude followed their surprise. Here was someone from outside Korea to record their struggles and successes. As I was about to tap the next shoulder ahead, I could also see in their eyes an expression of pride in what they'd achieved.

I was not able to keep up with the questions and comments that bombarded us from all sides, but it didn't seem to matter as long as we moved forward— even if we weren't sure where forward was.

"Where is the effigy of Chun Doo-hwan?" I asked.

"Over there, by the fountain," said a young woman as she pointed ahead.

Near the fountain, people sat cross-legged on the ground. The atmosphere here was the same as at the periphery of the crowd, where people stood instead of sat. There was no anger. There was only determination to right a wrong. They had achieved their first goal by pushing the hated soldiers out of town. All around me, young and old alike reveled in the fact that they were now in charge.

"No one in Korea believes us. If the rest of the world learns what happened here, they'll get behind us," said an older man who stood next to me.

"Take lots of pictures. If people in Seoul see your pictures, they'll support us," said his colleague. Robin was already set up and snapped photographs while I talked to curious onlookers.

"He's been taking many pictures, but it'll be many days before he can get out of Korea," I said, gesturing at Robin. I was still worried about how Robin would get out of Korea with his film. I could imagine the military confiscating his camera and film.

The effigy was lying in an ungainly position on the ground, the poor quality of its construction on conspicuous display. It appeared sad and forlorn. If this was the hated Chun Doo-hwan we had nothing to fear. A couple of people patched up the paper-and-wood structure. They tried to stand it up, only to have it collapse. It could not stand on its own and was not ready for burning. They worked on it, but it collapsed in a heap a few times before it was firmly affixed to a pole. A large cloth sash, like the ones the young people wore when they traveled to the periphery of town, adorned the effigy. "Chun Doo-hwan" was written in huge red letters. I figured that the sash may have been the most important part of the effigy, as I couldn't see any resemblance to Chun on the face.

Robin took more pictures as it was set afire. The entire crowd cheered with the gusto of fans at an American college football game. Chills raced up and down my spine as I listened. I found it amazing that these people continued to hold out against a far superior force. They so clearly believed that they were on the right side of history. Heck, *I* thought they were on the right side of history!

The flames died down quickly and the crowd started to sing the Korean national anthem, followed by a local protest song. The sound of ten thousand or more voices mesmerized me. Caught up in the mood of the moment, I had ignored Robin for the last ten to fifteen minutes. I glanced over at him and realized that he was probably as mesmerized as I was. We both stood, watched, and listened, and felt the crowd.

The songs came to an end and people started to disperse. Within a couple of minutes, a large group had collected around us. Questions and statements started flying so fast that I had to stop everyone.

"Please, one at a time, and slowly," I said. A couple of young men stepped forward.

"I was part of a group of three hundred university students from Seoul who came down to support Gwangju. We crossed into Gwangju near Damyang, but only about thirty of us made it. I don't know what happened to my friends. Were they captured by the soldiers?" said one of them.

"We heard that some students coming from Seoul were shot at from helicopters," said another.

"There was a bus with some old people from Hwasun trying to reach

Gwangju to find their children. We heard that soldiers shot at it," said a young woman.

The stories came too fast to keep track of. Some were first-person accounts, but others appeared to be rumors. It was impossible, in that short time and space, to separate the two. They related stories of helicopters shooting on civilians in Gwangju, and the vision of the *halmeoni* and young child in the mortuary resurfaced in my head. Everyone had a story—but how would the stories be captured and substantiated? I stared at the keen, animated faces surrounding us and wondered if the military government would ever allow these stories to be told.

"Why didn't the American government stop Chun from attacking?" asked one middle-aged man. The group became quiet. I didn't know how to respond and took a few seconds to compose my reply.

"I have not been able to call the US Embassy in Seoul. I don't think that they know what actually happened here," I said, then after a few more seconds, added, "We have seen what happened and, we'll tell them—and everyone we can." The man nodded his head, but his eyes told me that I had not answered his question.

Robin had his images. The group thinned, so we walked back to the front gate of the provincial office. The setting was becoming the new normal, starting to appear routine: young people picked up or dropped off weapons as they came from or went to defend the perimeter. *Halmeoni* continued to file into the mortuary to search for loved ones. No wailing ambulances interfered with these activities. I was grateful for that.

Dave and Terry waited for us at the bottom of the stairs to the provincial meeting room. Terry and Robin wanted to interview some of the student leaders. We walked into the room to be confronted by a passionate discussion. Two students, their voices raised, were adamant that they'd defend Gwangju to the end. The rest of the committee reiterated that they wanted to get Gwangju "back to normal." Food was becoming scarce and it seemed that the tension was exhausting people. I was exhausted. I turned to my colleagues.

"I'm going to try to get out of Gwangju again. It's too late today, so I'll try tomorrow," I said. I needed to do my bit, and let the US Embassy and the Peace Corps know what was really going on.

"How're you going to leave? You can't go by the roads," Dave said.

"Yeah, I know. I figure that if I go over the hills south of here I should be able to drop down on the other side into the area not far from Hohyewon," I said, as I outlined my thoughts. I'd been thinking about this route and was grateful that I'd hiked up the hills from the other side. I figured that all my summers of work in the forests of Idaho were going to be of value here. I'd learned how to "get the lay of the land" in order to plan how to get from point A to point B even if it involved some bushwhacking. Or, so I thought.

"Are there roads over those hills?" asked Dave.

"I don't think so. There should be some small ones that'll take me to the base of the hills, but from there I suspect I'll have to find footpaths or I'll end up bushwhacking," I said, with more confidence than I felt.

"The military is probably patrolling that area too," he countered.

"Yeah, I have to admit that the thought scares the hell out of me," I responded, not exactly sure if this was a good decision after all. "I can imagine the military shooting me, then saying something like, 'Look, the evil communist agitators in Gwangju have killed an American.'" I exhaled slowly. Was I nuts? Should I hunker down in Gwangju and wait?

"Do you think this is a wise decision?" Robin asked, adding to my unease. What could I say? Had decisions that I'd made up until now been wise?

"No idea. But it doesn't make sense to stay here anymore. One of us needs to get to Seoul to let Peace Corps and the embassy know what's actually happening here. I figure I know the lay of the land the best," I said. There were nods from Dave, Robin, and Terry, but nothing else was said. I had made a decision and now, I was more comfortable. At least I had a plan.

After a few minutes, the committee meeting broke up and we prepared to conduct two interviews. I sat with Robin and one student while Dave and Terry were with the other. The door flew open with a bang and two young men ran in. We jumped.

"The military is going to invade at six o'clock!" they yelled.

"That's only an hour from now," said Dave. The two young men ran out, to spread the news to other parts of the building. We kept the interviews short, just fifteen minutes. The interviews were a bit stilted, likely from the agitation in the room. It seemed to me that everyone in the room knew that the "invasion" would come, sooner or later. They, like me, hoped that it would be later. We wrapped up and Robin, Terry, and Dave went back to the hotel. I went the other direction, to Tim's house, to let him know about the rumored invasion and my plans to leave. The streets were quiet and I fast-walked as sweat creased its way down my back, a product of both the exertion and the stress.

I banged on the gate and the *ajumeoni* opened it. She looked me up and down, noticing my disheveled appearance, and her own face expressed concern. I found it difficult to express various emotions and decided to keep it simple. She accepted my "I'm okay" without probing. Inside I found Tim.

"Tim. While translating this afternoon at the provincial office we got a message that the military is planning to invade at six!"

"Six? We just heard that the invasion is going to be at five thirty!"

"Shit! Really? That's only fifteen minutes from now," I said, as I glanced at my watch. I continued in a rush, "Hey, tomorrow I'm going to try to get out—again. I'll come by in the morning and get my bike."

"How do you think you can get out?" Tim asked, as his hands waved in different directions. Ok-jin and his mother were the only others there and they both stared at us, probably wondering what was going on.

"I can't use the road, so I'm going to try to go over the mountain to Hohyewon," I said. The words rushed out of my mouth. "I'll fill you in tomorrow." I did a slight bow to the *ajumeoni* as she opened the gate and, instead of a fast-paced walk, I ran back to the hotel. It had become hard to separate fact from rumor over the last few days. I didn't want to test the truthfulness of the story about the military invasion. After a couple of blocks I was winded and switched to a fast walk down the nearly empty streets. My ears attuned to every sound and I found it impossible to restrain my imagination. Images from the day tumbled through my mind—was I going nuts? If a tank appeared, I would dive into the first *gage* or bang on the nearest gate.

I started to plot my "escape." I was already committed to joining the memorial service for those killed in order to translate for Robin in the morning. If I left Gwangju before noon I could make it home within eight hours. My bike would help me get across town to where I could start the climb. From there on, my bike was going to be a hindrance, particularly if the path dead-ended before I reached the ridge. If I had to, I'd abandon the bike on the hill. Still, if all went as planned, I figured that I'd be back home before dark. I conveniently excluded thoughts of what might happen if soldiers blocked my way, or worse.

I arrived back at the small hotel and learned from Robin and others that the "invasion" was another rumor. I dropped into a chair, in relief. Every sound in the last fifteen minutes had frayed my ragged nerves further.

"Your friend Dave has gone to the provincial building. He said he's going to spend the night there with the students," Robin announced, peering directly at me, probably wondering what my response would be.

"What? If the military invades tonight he could be killed!" I blurted out, sitting up straight, stunned.

"Yeah, we told him that was a possibility, but he was adamant," Robin replied with a shrug of his shoulders.

"Shit," was all I could muster, and I slumped back into my chair. I was completely out of sorts and at a loss for words. The reporters were sympathetic, and they sat with me for a bit and we ordered some food. The variety of fare had dropped, but there was still rice, dried seaweed, and kimchi. After we finished, I turned to the reporters.

"What do you guys think?"

"About what?" asked one of the Germans. "If you're asking about your friend staying with the students, I think that he's making a mistake. We've been in situations where, very quickly, things can go terribly wrong."

"Yeah, I know. While it's his decision to make, and I completely understand and support the moral argument, my fear is he's put the rest of us in an awkward position," I said, adding, "Now the military can say that we have become involved. And that strengthens their hand against us. They can kick us out of the country!" My head sank to nestle in my hands, elbows on the table to support them. I sat there for a minute and everyone was quiet. I then continued, "But I'm not going to the provincial office to try to talk him into coming back to the hotel. It's his decision."

"If you're worried about your plans to leave tomorrow, don't be. I suspect that tonight will pass calmly and Dave will be back tomorrow to translate for us. Tim said he'd join us in the afternoon for the press conference," said Terry.

"We're staying in Gwangju until the event is over. There'll be no footage, no photos—nothing out until we leave Korea," Robin added. "Given that martial law is in place, we may have difficulty getting our film out of the country."

"It'll be good if Peace Corps and the embassy can learn what's happened here. It's likely that the only perspective they're getting is that provided by Chun and his military," said Terry. "Try to get to Seoul and let them know."

"Thanks, guys," I said, sitting up straighter. I pointed to Robin. "I'll translate for you in the morning, then leave before noon."

"Thanks. Be careful. We all have seen what the military is capable of doing," Robin responded.

"Yep," I replied, my jaw clenched, and I regarded the reporters across from me. I had enjoyed working with these guys. I thought about how in the days, weeks, and months ahead we would have all gone separate ways, on divergent paths. I'd be back to my village while they'd be onto other assignments—that is, if everything went according to plan. I didn't want to think about how things might go wrong.

Day 12

Sunday, May 25:

Is there peace to be found heading over the mountain?

—

A light gentle rain overnight made the street glistening wet. Robin and I arrived at the provincial office to learn that the service planned for the morning had been canceled. The committee had decided that autopsies should be done on all of the bodies. The rain was only spitting now, but there were few people out. I wondered if the rain also contributed to the decision to cancel the service. Robin wanted pictures of a "service," so after talking with one of the student leaders, we were bundled into a car to go to a church. Three students, "impure elements" according to the military, hopped in the car with us. I had a momentary sense of discomfort about being in a car driven by a "rebel" and in the company of the students. The car was packed. I would have preferred to walk—even in the rain.

The students were keen to help us and we sped off down the clean, empty streets. I wondered where Dave was, after his night in the provincial building, but decided not to ask. I was afraid that the students would ask me to join them tonight. I would then have to find a way to say "no" without offending them.

We pulled up to a Catholic church. It was simple in design. Inside, a service was underway. There was no shouting, no crying, and no pounding on the pulpit. We stood at the back, not wanting to interrupt what seemed to be a typical Sunday service. Within ten minutes the service was over and people filed out the front, near to where we stood. Everyone wanted to pose for Robin. People were dressed in their Sunday best.

"There's nothing here to get a picture of. It looks like a Sunday church scene anywhere," Robin said, turning to me.

"Yep, it amazes me how normal everything appears and how normal everyone acts," I replied.

"People just want to get on with their lives," he sighed.

Before we could continue, a church leader came up to us, grabbed our hands, and led us to the back of the church. There, in a large room, jars of Maxwell House instant coffee and copper pots filled with boiling water sat out on tables. We were served coffee heavily laced with sugar and milk. To my surprise, I found the hot, sweet concoction comforting.

Congregants gathered around us and the "twenty questions" started. I managed to shift the focus of the questions from me to Robin: "Are you married? How many children do you have? How old are you? Where are you from? What are your hobbies?" He gamely answered and I translated. He glanced at me out of the corner of his eye and winked. I laughed. He knew that I'd shifted the questions over to him.

No one talked about the uprising, the precarious state they were in, or Chun Doo-hwan. It seemed that, this being Sunday church time, the challenges of the rest of the world were being set aside.

A couple of people offered us lunch, even though it was still early. I was overwhelmed by their generosity. But soon guilt crept in—I felt bad drinking their coffee and eating their pastries when I knew that food supplies were really tight.

We emerged from the church to find that our driver and "impure element compatriots" had waited for us. Robin and I packed back in the car, cheek to jowl, for the ride back to the provincial office. Our escorts wanted to know where else they could take us. As kindly as possible, I let them know that we had no further plans requiring transport.

I extracted myself, legs stiff, from the car. One of the student leaders ran up to us from the provincial office gate.

"Mr. Kim, who you interviewed yesterday, and another man on the civilian committee have been stabbed," he said.

"What?" I asked, stunned by the announcement.

"They were stabbed with a ballpoint pen," he said.

"Really? Who did it?" I asked, still a bit dazed.

"Someone in Gwangju who was angry. We really don't know. He wasn't a soldier," he added.

"Are they alright?" I asked. I then wondered if being stabbed with a pen was likely to be life-threatening. "Where are they?"

"They'll be okay. They're at Jeonnam University Hospital," he said, agitated. This seemed like a small incident, but it added to the general sense of paranoia that circulated in people around me. I was also starting to feel paranoid. I glanced over my shoulder, wondering when the next incident would happen—when the soldiers would attack.

The clouds had dispersed and the sun dried the pavement. Last night's rain was probably too little to make the paths over the hills muddy. The sun would dry the trails I would have to use in the afternoon. I walked back to the small hotel with Robin to bid farewell to the journalists.

"Guys, I'm heading out now. I'll try to go over the hills," I said, pointing in the direction I was heading. "I guess you'll see me again this afternoon if I get turned back," I added with a shrug of my shoulders. I was scared, but I didn't want to show it.

"Paul, you need to be really careful. You've seen what the military has done—what they can do," said Robin.

"Yeah, I'll be careful. If I see any soldiers I'll just turn back. It was a pleasure to translate for you. I really hope you can get the story out," I said to all of them. They nodded. Many things seemed out of my control. I just needed to move forward with my own plan. My responsibilities as a witness had evolved. Observing was one thing. Writing it all down to share was another. Translating so that the voices of the unheard could be heard was yet another. Reporters seemed to have figured out their roles: when to observe and document, when to intervene to assist, and when to intervene to make sure something bad didn't happen. I wasn't there yet.

I was out the door within a few minutes and walked toward Tim's place to get my bike. As I walked, my thoughts wandered. If I'd been born Korean and in Gwangju instead of in the US, would I have been willing to take up the struggle against Chun Doo-hwan? Would I risk my life as all of these young people continued to do? I was uneasy with these questions. Growing up an American, I believed my voice counted and that my leaders were accountable. I knew I was privileged by the simple fact that I was born in the US—it had nothing to do with me. These young people, putting their lives on the line for what they felt was right and just, were born in a dictatorship. They wanted a voice in their future. I wondered if my country was willing to stand by them.

It was late morning when I got to Tim's place. The rain had stopped hours before and the pavement was dry. My pack, slung over one shoulder, held everything I had arrived with earlier in the week. My clothes desperately needed a wash. Ok-jin opened the gate and it struck me that he'd not left his house since the uprising started. I found Tim inside on the floor, helping the *ajumeoni* with cleaning.

"Hey, Tim, I'm getting my bike and will head out," I said. "If all goes as planned, I should be in Hohyewon by this evening."

"And from there?" he asked, lifting his head as he squatted on his haunches.

"Well, if that works, I'll go up to Seoul tomorrow."

"Man, I hope that works," he said.

"I have some bad news." I paused, as Tim looked alarmed. "Dave spent last night in the provincial office," I announced, with my hands on my hips.

"What!" Tim shouted and shot upright. "He's lucky the military didn't move in last night." His response was what I expected.

"Yeah, and if he stays there again tonight…" I said, catching myself before I completed the sentence. I didn't like any of the potential outcomes. Tim continued to stare at me.

"Do the reporters still need translation?" he asked, shaking his head.

"Yep, I think that they'll need help with the press conference planned for this afternoon. I hope Dave shows up."

"Are you okay with your plan to hike over the hills?" Tim asked, concern in his voice.

"Not really, but I don't see any other options," I said. Tim and I hugged. I needed to go.

The *ajumeoni* opened the gate for me and I lifted my bike over the threshold. She didn't offer boiled eggs this time. I was already prepared to refuse if she did.

The roads were serenely quiet and the only reminder of the earlier rain was an occasional puddle of water. It was an easy ride through the outskirts of Gwangju. There were very few people out. I kept my bike pointed toward the base of the hills south of town. I'd not been this way before, but I figured that there must be a path up to the ridgeline. Slowly, steadily, I took one small back street after another until I ended up on a dirt road that seemed to lead to the base of the hills—directly where I thought I should start up and over. The small farming plots were interspersed with older houses, some still with a thatched roof. I felt that I was truly in the most rural part of the city.

I reached the end of the dirt road. Earlier I had passed a few people walking on the road, but there had been no one for the last kilometer or so. There was a small rustic house on the right and the start of a decent-sized path on the left. Chickens were creating a racket in the yard, so I knew someone lived there. I banged on the metal gate.

"*Yeoboseyo*," I called.

"Eh," came a tentative reply from inside. The voice sounded like that of an old woman, so I continued.

"*Halmeoni*, I want to walk over the mountain."

Her next "Eh?" was less tentative. "Why would you want to do that?"

A smile crept across my face and I wanted to laugh. Instead, I said, "I want to go to my home near Nampyeong." I knew that no one beyond five kilometers of Hohyewon had heard of the place, and it seemed pointless to mention it and confuse her.

It was hard talking to a gate. There was silence, and I wondered if she'd open the gate or would even respond. I waited. Finally, there was a response.

"There's a path that will take you to the top of the mountain," she replied, then added, "There are paths down on the other side."

"Thank you, *halmeoni.*" Although I was still talking to the gate I bowed slightly, out of habit.

I crossed the dirt road and checked out the pathway. It was wide enough for one of the ubiquitous motorized carts that crawled through rural fields all over Korea, so it was wide enough for me to walk my bike. I started up, traversed the hillside, and passed several small terraced vegetable plots. Bamboo frames, in a half-moon shape, covered some of the plots, and I knew that in a few weeks they would be covered with plastic to make them into greenhouses. The motorized carts also served as tractors, which explained why the pathway remained wide. After twenty minutes, the pathway forked, with one narrow section continuing up and a wider path continuing across. I went up, confident that I was headed in the right direction.

The rain had stopped at least five hours earlier but, as I got higher, its lingering effects, particularly in shaded areas, made for slippery mud instead of the hard-packed dirt I'd hoped for. Both my shoes and my bike tires started to cake up. I stopped to inspect the path for other footprints and found none. I continued on and tried to figure out what the lack of footprints meant. It could be that this path was no longer used and was going to end and I would have to find another way. Or it could mean that there were no soldiers in this area. My shirt was already damp from the exertion and the thought of soldiers produced more beads of sweat. What I did conclude was that there was no one here I could ask for directions.

I slogged upward, occasionally having to carry my bike on my shoulder when the path narrowed too much. I was grateful that I could walk it most of the time. I came across a couple of vegetable terraces, much smaller than the ones lower down. I also came across the first of several burial mounds, which brought me back to the sights and sounds in the temporary mortuary. Although seared into my brain, that place now seemed like a million miles away. I hiked on and gained elevation. My heart was beating fast, in equal measure due to the uphill slog and the "hair on the back of my neck" feel that the military might be lurking. Around every bend in the pathway and behind every burial mound I imagined some soldiers who would block my way. I simply wanted to get home.

Almost three hours after talking to the *halmeoni*, I reached the ridgeline. I was pleased to see, down the other side, the small river that eventually made its way to Nampyeong. My shoes, pants, and bike were all coated in mud. I walked my bike along the ridgetop and continued to search for footprints in the dirt. There were none. The area was not heavily forested and I followed the ridgeline east. After about an hour, I found the trail leading down to Hohyewon and I dropped over the crest.

My thoughts crested too. I was now outside Gwangju and away from the soldiers, their weapons, and their massive tanks. I was also away from the coffins, the silenced young man wearing the bloodied sash, and the distraught parents and grandparents.

The path down was not as muddy or exhausting as the slog coming up. I was tired and hungry, but I knew I needed to keep going.

I staggered into Hohyewon around seven. It was a Sunday evening and I was not surprised that there was no one out. I parked my mud-splattered bike next to my room, unlocked the door, and dropped my bag inside. I stood outside a moment, eyes unfocused, reflecting on the last week. Instead of going in, I decided to go to the house of Mr. Kim, the village leader, to let him know I was back.

"*Yeoboseyo*," I said, as I knocked on his door.

"Mr. Ko! Come in!" he boomed, his eyes wide with surprise. He looked up and down at the mud encrusted on my pants and shoes. I decided that it was best not to enter, so I stood in front of his doorway.

"The Peace Corps office called. I told them you were in Gwangju," he said.

"The phone works?" I asked in surprise.

"Yes, the phone started working again yesterday," he continued, taking a puff of his cigarette. "They want you to call them immediately."

I was wondering what "immediately" meant. "Okay. Should I call them tonight or wait till morning?" I asked.

Without an answer, he stepped outside, put out his cigarette, slipped into his shoes, and closed the door. We walked to the village office—the one place in the village where I didn't have to take off my shoes. He didn't ask me any questions as we walked. I suspected that the state of my clothes, the weariness in my eyes, and the slowness of my pace told him what he needed to know. I turned to him.

"All of the students on the list you gave me are okay. The *ajumeoni* at my friend's house called all of them," I said. He nodded his thanks.

At the office, Mr. Kim unlocked the phone and dialed. I sank into a chair and felt like I could just melt away. He handed the receiver to me. I couldn't imagine that anyone would be at the Peace Corps office on a Sunday evening. I didn't recognize the voice on the other end. On hearing my name, the speaker gave me the phone number of the Peace Corps director and said that I was to call him immediately. I did as instructed.

"Hi, this is Paul Courtright."

"Paul! Am I glad to hear your voice! Where are you? How are you? How are Tim, Dave, Julie, and Judi?" Jim's voice boomed down the line and I held the receiver away from my ear. His questions came fast and furious. How could I respond to all of them? I took a deep breath.

"We're all fine. Everyone is still trapped in Gwangju. I just got out today."

"Are you safe?"

"Yes, I'm safe," I said. "I'm in my village. The roads in and out of Gwangju are blocked and I had to walk over the hills to get out."

"Can you travel?" he asked. "You should come to Seoul tomorrow. Use whatever form of transport you need. You'll be reimbursed."

"I'll try. The military has Gwangju completely blockaded. They're not

letting anyone in or out. I don't know the situation for the rest of Jeonnam."
I paused, thinking. "I'll try to get to my health center in Naju tomorrow
morning and see if they can help."

"When you get to Seoul, call me."

"Do you know what happened here?" I asked. Without waiting for
an answer, I continued. "The military killed hundreds of people, maybe
thousands—men, women, and children. It was a massacre. What you've
seen on Korean TV is not true. There are no communist sympathizers.
Chun Doo-hwan caused this, not the people of Gwangju!" My voice rose
and I gripped the phone as if it were a weapon. I was ready to unload even
more, but Jim cut me off.

"I want you to come to Seoul as soon as you can. Go to the embassy. I'll
meet you there. You can tell them everything that you've seen," he said.

I had held my breath while he talked. I wanted to understand every single
word he said. I let it out with a sense of relief. From his words and voice, I
had the sense that Jim withheld judgment, and that he believed me. I wanted
him to hear our story and understand the reasons for the decisions we had
made. I knew that the Korean military narrative would be the national
narrative. I didn't want that account to be accepted by the Peace Corps. I
was less sure about our ability to influence the US government narrative.

I slowly put the phone back in its cradle. I felt completely drained. Mr.
Kim did not rush me. After a minute he reached over, closed the wood box
in which the phone rested, and locked it. I turned to him. He was watching
me with concern in his eyes.

He had not understood the conversation I had with Jim, but the words
Gwangju, Chun Doo-hwan, and Seoul got his attention. He wanted to know
my plans.

"Tomorrow morning I'll go to the Naju Health Center. I'll ask them to
help me to get to Seoul," I said, my voice still shaky.

"The buses still aren't running," he said, "But you can get a ride from
anyone on the roads. They'll help you."

"I hope so," I sighed. I said my goodbyes and did a bow. He took my
hand. He'd never touched me before and our eyes met.

"Travel safely. Tell them what you saw."

"Thank you. I understand," was all I could manage. I choked up.

Unlocking my door again, I took off my shoes. I also took off my pants before entering—I didn't care if anyone saw me. I stood in the doorway in my underwear and surveyed my room. It appeared small and insignificant, but it felt safe and welcoming.

I popped a James Taylor cassette into my player and put on sweats. I was starving. I turned on my little burner and made ramen. It was the quickest and easiest thing to make. I cracked two eggs, stirring them in as the noodles boiled. It tasted better than any meal I could remember.

I took clothing out of my pack while my mind drifted. What was going on when I last wore this dirty shirt or this pair of pants? Images inundated my brain and thoughts cascaded through my consciousness. I worried about my friends in Gwangju. I worried about myself. I worried that no one would know what happened in Gwangju. I worried that I would fail. I felt lost.

I sat down and started a letter to my parents, relating the events, but after a few minutes, I stopped. I couldn't send this. Writing to friends about what had happened was okay, but it was not something for Mom and Dad. I tore up the letter.

I warmed some water on my burner and took a sponge bath. The mud stuck to my pants and bike would have to wait until after I got back from Seoul. Both were outside my room, so I didn't have to see them. Right now, I just wanted to be clean.

I packed for the morning, wondering if and when I'd be back. Then I sat and wrote, and wrote, and wrote. Writing helped to quell my anxiety about the past week and the coming day. The writing was only for me. James Taylor's "Up on the Roof" played, and the words and tune made me feel far from home. I wanted to be "up on the roof" somewhere. I wanted everything to be clear.

Day 13

Monday, May 26:

Losing my temper and heading to Seoul

—

I checked my stuff for the trip and glanced around the room—how long would I be gone? Should I try to get my slide film processed in Seoul? I had no idea what the military clampdown meant outside Jeonnan Province. My paranoia returned in full force. Was I a target?

As I stepped outside my door, I nearly collided with my mud-encrusted bike. Off to the right, my pants still hung on a hook. They were both just going to have to stay as they were until I got back. I needed my shoes, however, and set to scraping the hard-packed mud off the soles. The sound and smell of thousands of chickens, going about their business of making the village wealthy, which I normally felt assaulted by, calmed me. This was just another normal day in Hohyewon. If it were truly a normal day for me, I would've started my rounds and checked in on patients. As it was, I had no idea if the two men I had taken for their eyelid surgery had returned from the hospital. No, this was not a normal day.

I strode to the village office. Mr. Kim and I kept our greetings and farewells brief. It seemed to me that he was keen to get back to the more prosaic, but essential, task of village economic growth. I was now on foot and needed to hitch a ride—it was either hitch a ride or walk the entire way to Naju. In rapid order, I had rides, first in a small pickup to Nampyeong and then in a car to Naju. The absence of buses seemed to make drivers willing to help out anyone on the road.

In Naju the car pulled over and I got out in front of the gutted police station. Although charred, the building had been cleaned out. Naju seemed to be in the first phase of recovery.

I walked into the health center and climbed the stairs to the large open office. I was immediately surrounded by half a dozen of my colleagues. It felt like months had passed since I was last here, instead of a few days. My leprosy coworker, the Maternal & Child Health worker and her assistant, the TB worker, and various other folks, some of whom I didn't recognize, all clustered around me in a tight semicircle. I didn't see Miss Kim and figured that she was still stuck in Gwangju. They sat me down, pulled up their own chairs, and peppered me with questions. Even the new, young doctor who had recently become the health center director came out of his office and joined the group. The questions came fast and I couldn't keep up to respond to each.

"Stop! Wait," I said. "I'll tell you everything I can—with all the details. Let's just go slowly." They quieted down. I took a breath and gazed up at the ceiling for a few seconds. Everyone waited. I started my story with the bike ride into Gwangju, the soldiers and roadblocks, the buses, and trying to leave with Miss Kim. When I mentioned her there were a couple of gasps and the shaking of heads. Then I got to the part about translating for the journalists. Talking about the bodies in the temporary mortuary turned out to be more difficult than I had imagined. I pictured again the grief-stricken *halmeoni* on their knees next to coffins and my voice cracked. I struggled unsuccessfully to keep my composure as my heart felt that it was being torn into little bits. I couldn't keep eye contact with the listeners around me as a film of tears blurred my vision.

Mr. Chen, the TB worker, started laughing.

I lost it. Something quite different cracked inside. I had been holding all the horror, pain, and anger I'd witnessed over the last week. It just gave way.

I erupted.

"What are you laughing about?" I yelled at Mr. Chen. "I saw Koreans— *halmeoni* and children—who had been killed! They were dead! The soldiers killed hundreds of people." Hot tears started to leak from the corners of my eyes and I stared at Mr. Chen. I shut my mouth, my shoulders heaved, and the room became deathly silent. Mr. Chen sat woodenly, ashen-faced. I'd never lost my temper in Korea. It just wasn't done, and with my outburst, I had just lost face. The embarrassment in the room could have been cut with a knife. I didn't care. How dare he laugh!

The health center director stood up. "Mr. Ko, let's go into my office," I heard him say through a fog. I got up, stiffly with my head hanging down, and followed him. The large room remained silent as I shuffled into his office. He closed the door behind me and we sat down. My shoulders heaved from the emotional outburst and, gazing down, I could see my hands shaking. I was exhausted. He peered at me, forcing me to look him directly in the eye.

"Don't think badly of Mr. Chen. He wasn't laughing at you and he wasn't laughing about what happened in Gwangju. He was laughing because he was embarrassed. We want foreigners to see only the good things in Korea. You've seen some of the bad things," he said.

"I'm sorry," I said softly, still breathing deeply as I tried to regain my composure. I wanted to find a way to distance myself from the anger I'd felt. I sat up straighter and continued to gaze at him directly.

"Don't feel sorry," he said. "We're the ones who are sorry. What happened in Gwangju is horrible. We cannot go back to the way things were before." His voice was calm and measured. "It's important that you were a witness. We all have many friends and family in Gwangju. We're all angry. We're all afraid."

His words penetrated my fog of anger and embarrassment. While it made sense to me, given what I had learned about the Korean culture, I struggled to reconcile my feelings with my coworker's laughter. I thought about Miss Kim—was she okay? I tried to sit up straighter and wiped my eyes with my sleeve.

"Has the military invaded Gwangju?" I asked, as my voice gained strength.

"Not yet, but we expect it will happen shortly. We've seen more military vehicles move toward Gwangju. They're massing on all of the main roads. They're not letting anyone enter or leave," he said. "The TV still talks about Gwangju in a bad way."

He regarded me and stroked his chin. "But, you made it out." He smiled faintly. For the first time, I felt like I was no longer just the American assigned to them. I was one with them. "That's important," he continued. "Because people outside of Jeonnam don't know what really happened."

I gazed out his large window toward the burned-out police station, then back at him. I leaned forward. "I need to go to Seoul. I had a call from the Peace Corps director last night. He said he'll meet me at the US Embassy. I can tell them what really happened," I said, my confidence somewhat restored by his words.

"Good," he said. He sat back, tapped his chin with a pen, and continued to stare at me. I waited. "Getting out of Jeonnam will not be easy. All of the main roads are blocked. No one is allowed to leave. Some of the small roads are open, but there are many roadblocks. All young people trying to leave are being taken prisoner. As an American, it will be easier for you."

"What do you suggest?" I asked.

"Wait a few minutes. I may be able to help you. I know a man who has a taxi. He could drive you north to Jeonju. You can get the bus to Seoul from there. He's originally from Gwangju. I'll find out how much it will cost. Do you have money to pay him and the bus?"

"Yes, I have money. Thank you," I said.

He turned and started to dial. After a couple of minutes of rapid talking on the phone, he turned back to me.

"It's sorted out. He'll take you to Jeonju," he said.

"Thank you." I shifted uncomfortably in my chair. "Will you please give my apology to everyone?" I asked as I pointed toward the door. I felt both fortunate and grateful for this man's understanding, but I was also embarrassed. Had I ruined my relationship with my coworkers?

"There's no need for an apology," he replied, looking at me squarely.

I got up and left the office. The room I stepped back into was quiet. Everyone was back at work. I would have liked a hug, but giving hugs, like outbursts of temper, was not a Korean trait. I went to the desk they had assigned me over a year ago and rifled through the drawers for something to do while I waited for the taxi.

When my coworkers glanced up from their work, one by one, I saw their tentative smiles. I felt supported. My outburst didn't seem to have had the damaging effect I'd feared. Maybe, in those twenty minutes that I was with the director, I'd even ceased being the crazy Peace Corps Volunteer living in a village of leprosy patients. I was now *their* crazy Peace Corps Volunteer.

I heard a car horn downstairs and, in a few seconds, the director came out of his office. My coworkers waved goodbye and we both went downstairs. A small green taxi was idling and the driver stepped out. While I stood there he and my director talked, out of my earshot. Within a minute they were done. I opened the back door of the taxi and got in. Through the open window, the director handed me a couple of packets of biscuits and some juice for the journey. Our farewells were brief and we pulled away from the health center on a virtually empty road.

A few minutes after we left Naju, the driver stopped and turned to me.

"Sit in the front seat," he said. I did as instructed.

"Every time we get to a roadblock there'll be many cars. If we wait in line you'll never get to Seoul. I want you to sit in the front so everyone can see you," he said, as he pulled back onto the road.

"I understand," I said, while I shifted uneasily in my seat. His clear and unambiguous instructions suggested to me that he knew what he was talking about. I had the sense that he had not been sitting at home during the last two weeks.

I wasn't sure the man would want to identify himself, but I still felt I should make an attempt at the basic courtesies.

"My name is Ko Seong-cheol," I said.

"I'm Moon Sung-nam," he responded, while he continued to gaze straight ahead. Mr. Moon must have been about forty years of age and his hands, stained with oil and grease, suggested that he both maintained and drove his vehicle. He was his own boss. Most Korean men didn't wear wedding rings, so I had no idea if he was married or not. The taxi gave no indication of religious affiliation or of a family. His face was still smooth, and not unfriendly, but he was not a man you would want to cross.

As I settled into the front seat I thought about my current state. I had handed over complete control of my situation to the unknown Mr. Moon. Strangely, that had a calming effect on me. His brusque take-charge attitude was comforting right now, and I was ready to do whatever he told me.

On a small back road, about twenty kilometers northwest of Naju, we came to a long line of cars. Way ahead we could see some soldiers. I turned to Mr. Moon for orders.

"Stick your head out the window and say 'American,'" he fired at me. "I am going to pull around all the cars." He obviously expected me to obey without question and I did.

As he pulled out around the cars, I leaned out until almost half of my body was outside the window. I yelled, over and over again. I felt like an idiot. Three soldiers turned, their weapons pointed directly at us. One gestured angrily for us to get back in line.

I continued yelling and Mr. Moon continued driving forward, although more slowly. More soldiers surrounded us as we neared the roadblock, yelling at Mr. Moon. I jumped out of the taxi. Sweat beaded on my brow and trickled down my neck.

"I'm an American. I work for the US Embassy. I have to go to Seoul!" I shouted, and walked slowly but determinedly toward one of the soldiers. He and others all wore the same damn sunglasses. I wanted to snatch them off his face and smash them underfoot. I worked at trying to keep my fists from clenching.

As I continued to walk forward, I saw about a half-dozen young men on the left side of the road. They sat cross-legged on the ground, their heads bowed, handcuffed and guarded. All looked tired and ragged. I tried not to stare; instead, I gave all of my attention to the soldier with his gun pointed at me.

"I'm sorry. I'm an American. I work for the US Embassy. I have to go to Seoul," I repeated, no longer as a shout. I stood there, stared at the soldier, and wanted desperately to stand firm.

He hesitated for a few seconds. "Go," he said, using his rifle to point in the direction we were heading. Mr. Moon put the car into gear and pulled up. I jumped back in, nearly collapsing with relief. He weaved through the roadblock as I ignored the stares of soldiers and other travelers stuck in line.

"Good," Mr. Moon said, with a nod of his head at me. "We'll have to do that a few more times," he added, and shifted into a higher gear.

"Did you see those young men?" I asked, with a tilt of my head back in the direction we'd come from.

Mr. Moon grunted and shifted his body slightly. I started to wonder again about him. He seemed too young to have a child at the university. He didn't appear to be afraid of the soldiers and his confidence infected me. I was grateful for the aura of safety he exuded. At the same time, I didn't like to play the foreigner card and get special treatment. It left a bad taste in my mouth. People were going to be stuck there for a long time, answering questions and having their cars searched. More young people would be taken away.

Mr. Moon slammed on the brakes, and I was yanked out of my thoughts. The tires squealed and my seat belt bit into my shoulder. I glanced up and saw a half-dozen soldiers run down the slope on our right—straight at us with their rifles aimed at our chests. I unbuckled my seat belt as fast as I could and jumped out of the car, momentarily wishing that I had blond hair.

I put my hands out in front in a defensive manner. "I'm an American. I work for the US Embassy in Seoul," I said, in the strongest voice I could manage. My sweat-soaked shirt was plastered to my back. Almost instantly I was in the middle of a ring of soldiers with guns pointed at me.

"Show me your ID," the lead soldier barked. Mr. Moon got out of the car and we both handed cards over. He turned my ID over a couple of times.

"This says 'Peace Corps,' not 'US Embassy,'" the soldier said, facing me with those damn reflecting sunglasses. My hands had a slight tremor. I crossed my arms over my chest to keep them hidden.

"Peace Corps is part of the US government. Peace Corps is part of the US Embassy," I responded, while I shifted my weight from one foot to the other to appear more authoritative than I felt. I hadn't anticipated being questioned by soldiers. He looked us over again as he fondled our IDs. Another soldier opened the doors and searched inside the taxi.

"Open the trunk," a third soldier growled and Mr. Moon complied, slowly and deliberately. The other soldiers still surrounded us, their gun barrels only a few meters away. I stood still, frozen to the spot.

After what seemed like an eternity, the soldier handed our IDs back and waved us on without another word being uttered. I gratefully sank into my seat and buckled my seat belt. Mr. Moon exhaled through his mouth as he shifted gears and we slowly passed by the soldiers. I peeked in the side-view mirror and saw that their weapons were still pointed at us. Mr. Moon and I exchanged glances. Both of us were shaky. I felt a bond with this man.

There were two more roadblocks before we crossed into Jeonbuk Province, but we had our act down. I kept my window open and hand on my seat belt, ready to release it and jump out of the car. Using the back roads and negotiating the roadblocks meant that it was almost five hours before Mr. Moon pulled into the Jeonju bus station. By then, it was afternoon and the sun had warmed both me and the landscape throughout the day. The atmosphere in Jeonju felt like "day" to Gwangju's "night." Jeonju was calm and relaxed, as if nothing had been happening in the province next door. We found the bus station and I went inside to buy a ticket. The next bus to Seoul would leave in thirty minutes. I stared up at the board with the bus schedule and saw that all buses to Gwangju were canceled.

I went out and sat back in the taxi with Mr. Moon. He slowly unwound his body and told me that he had relatives living nearby. He would spend the night there before trying to get back to Naju.

"Be safe, Mr. Ko," he said. His eyes could have pierced me.

"Thanks, Mr. Moon. You're a great driver," I said, with a real sense that this man, with whom I'd spent the last few hours, had become an important person in my life. "Stay safe on your way back to Naju. Thank the health center director for me," I added. I gave Mr. Moon the agreed fare. Tipping is not practiced in Korea and he would have been offended if I tried, but I'd have happily paid double the amount.

Mr. Moon nodded. "I will. He told me to call him when we got here," he said. His eyes revealed an unspoken awareness that impressed me.

"Really?" was all I could say.

"He also told me to remind you to tell the US Embassy what you saw in Gwangju."

That was the first time he had mentioned Gwangju. Now I was even more intrigued by Mr. Moon. There must be more to him that he hadn't told me. I couldn't blame him. I wasn't going to probe.

"I'm going straight to the US Embassy when I get to Seoul," I said. "Thanks for bringing me here."

I bowed my farewell, slung my pack on my shoulder, and went to the Seoul-bound bus, which filled up in a few minutes. I found my seat next to the window and we were off.

*   *   *

I was too wound up to nap and spent most of the trip with my eyes fixed on the view out the window. It was only ten days ago that I was on this same road. Then I was on my way home, through Gwangju. It seemed like a former life.

I couldn't observe the trees, farmhouses, temples, and people in the same way as before. Gwangju had changed that. The conversations on the bus were muted, but I never heard the word "Gwangju." I wasn't surprised when the bus stopped about thirty minutes outside of Jeonju. It was a roadblock. Soldiers boarded and demanded to see everyone's IDs. Two young men on the bus were pulled off. I stared out the window as they were forced to sit on the ground under guard. There were already a half-dozen young men there, some handcuffed. All had their heads bowed.

My hostile stare at the soldier who checked my ID was ignored. I was insignificant. I was helpless. I wanted to open the window and scream at the young men, "Keep your heads up! People in Gwangju are proud of you! I'm proud of you!" I kept the window closed.

It was dark by the time the bus reached Seoul. I found the bank of orange phones, inserted ten won coins, and called Jim. I told him that it would take me about thirty minutes to get to the embassy, so we planned to meet there around eight thirty. As I boarded the city bus, I rehearsed my account of what happened. Each day was imprinted on my brain. I had also memorized what Tim told me about the events of May 18. A few days ago in Gwangju, Tim, Judi, Dave, and I had agreed to avoid speculation and only tell what we saw ourselves. It was now up to me. If asked, I would not speculate on how many people were killed, why the military attacked, or why the military pulled out. I figured that time would provide those answers.

The US Embassy is a nondescript four-story building. It's not much to look at; what it has going for it is the location. It sits in the most central part of Seoul, across from the magnificent Sejong Cultural Center and down the street from the imposing Gyeongbok Palace. It's right in the heart of the city. The bus dropped me off and I walked the short distance to the embassy. I stood outside the gate and waited for Jim.

Jim arrived by taxi, greeted me, and gave me a hug. I didn't expect the hug but was grateful for it. We were ushered inside and led to the Chargé d'Affairs' office. Jim had made an appointment. My confidence was strong that the story I had to tell was important. The embassy must be hungering for eyewitness accounts. Even though it was evening, the embassy was abuzz with activity. We sat outside the Chargé d'Affairs' office for the next two hours.

No one ever came. We got up and left.

I was shocked. How were they going to understand what really happened?

Now, with this book, I'm finally telling the story the *halmeoni* wanted to be heard.

Epilogue

—

Around four in the morning of May 27, the military invaded Gwangju and the "Gwangju Uprising" came to an end. The following day I went with a Peace Corps staff member to Gwangju to pick up my friends and bring them to Seoul. All were safe.

While in Seoul I talked about Gwangju to any Peace Corps Volunteer I found. I was disheartened—they had no other source of information and had accepted the military narrative. The five of us drafted our accounts for the Peace Corps and tried to get on with our lives. That was not easy. I continued to have difficulty sleeping, as my brain ran through the events of each day. I traveled to Taiwan and holed up in a small guesthouse at the southernmost point of the island and I rewrote everything, one day at a time. Once I was finished, sleep came more readily.

I returned to Hohyewon. Mr. Kim, my village leader, met me with a letter he had from the military government. It said I was to be "protected" and that there would be a soldier posted to watch my movements. The letter also stated that I had to provide Mr. Kim with a detailed schedule of where I was going and when. He would pass this on to the military authorities. I dutifully complied, mainly because I didn't want to cause Mr. Kim any trouble. Both he and I knew that I had been designated an "impure element."

About a month later, I learned that the military government had demanded that those of us who were in Gwangju and translated for the reporters be expelled from the country. The Peace Corps director called their bluff and they backed down. I stayed.

My father died in late 1980. In mid-1981, Peace Corps Korea closed its doors for good. I had completed my Peace Corps service by then but I was not ready to leave Korea, so I took a job teaching at Seoul International School. Why did I stay? In September 1982, I packed up my bags and boarded a flight to leave Korea. I had grown to love the country, its people, and its history, even though some of that history was painful.

Chun Doo-hwan's military government continued to squash any alternative narratives about Gwangju. Stories remained unheard.

In the US, I went to graduate school and completed my doctorate in epidemiology and public health. In the late 1980s and early 1990s, along with my wife, I returned to Korea a number of times to undertake, with Korean colleagues, research and training related to the eye complications of leprosy. It was enjoyable work, but it was not a time to talk about Gwangju.

Why did it take me almost forty years to pull up my notes, letters, and other material and write? I can find many excuses but, simply put, remembering Gwangju was painful and I wanted to get on with my life. I've had a wonderful career, and my wife and I worked in various countries in Africa for twenty years. Our sons grew up there.

It was not until much later that I realized that the uprising, now referred to as 5.18 (the date of the first massacre), was the birth of the democratic movement in Korea. There are people, far more knowledgeable than I, who have documented the events.

My stimulation for writing this memoir was twofold. First, I sought to have a narrative of the event that Westerners, particularly Americans, might be interested to read. Few people in the West are familiar with the event— one of the reasons being that the eruption of Mt. St. Helens in Washington state literally blew the reports of Gwangju off the news in May 1980. Second, I realized that I still had unresolved psychological issues that I thought could be addressed by the task of writing this memoir. The upcoming fortieth anniversary of the event, to be in May 2020, was an extra stimulus.

I returned to Korea in May 2019 to visit 5.18 sites to make sure that I'd captured them correctly in this book. I spent a couple of weeks in Gwangju, Nampyeong, and Hohyewon after a week in Seoul. While in Seoul, I was shocked to realize that Chun Doo-hwan's narrative of 1980 still holds sway among some Koreans today. Although there are numerous academic pieces on 5.18, the full range of stories about the entire period remains uncaptured and, as a result, unheard. After a number of requests for newspaper and TV interviews, I was told that Koreans needed to hear the story from a foreigner who was in Gwangju during 5.18 as our stories were considered more "objective." While I tried to maintain objectivity during the events and in my retelling, the mere fact that these atrocities were committed makes it impossible for me not to be furious with those high up in the military. In addition, my understanding and appreciation of the people's desire to live in a country that respected them as full members grew. Apologies are important and for many years, no apologies were offered. I'm pleased that has changed.

America failed Korea and Koreans in 1980. I only hope that as an American writing this, both Americans and Koreans will better appreciate our shared history, our shared desires, and our shared pain. We have so much to learn from each other—I'm continuing to learn.

Acknowledgments

—

Writing this memoir would not have been possible without the support and editorial assistance of my wife, Dr. Susan Lewallen. I'm also grateful to my sons, James Courtright and Tom Courtright, for their input. Additional thanks go to Suzanne Crowder-Han, Jan Lewallen, Matt VanVolkenburg, Park So-yeon, Han Yunsok, and Joy Kim for their helpful comments. Lisa Wolff was my editor and I'm grateful for all of her helpful comments and edits. Any errors in the story I have tried to capture are purely my own.

All royalties from the sale of the book will go to support the important prevention of blindness work carried out by the Kilimanjaro Centre for Community Ophthalmology (www.kcco.net).

Annex

Annex 1. US Embassy Cable: Insider's Account of Kwangju Riot

This US Embassy cable to the US State Department, dated June 10, 1980, is a missionary's account of the Gwangju Uprising. There were three missionary families in Gwangju. This cable was presumably written by John Thomas Underwood. Pages 7-8 refer to the Peace Corps Volunteers' action. This part appeared in a chapter written by John Underwood's wife, Jean Marie Welch Underwood, in *Contentious Kwangju: The May 18 Uprising in Korea's Past and Present* (2003). As this document predates the Korean government's change to the Revised Romanization system in 2000, Gwangju appears as Kwangju, Daejeon as Taejon, and Gyeongsang as Kyongsang.

ADP246

PAGE 01   SEOUL 07402   01 OF 10   101321Z
ACTION EA-12

INFO   OCT-01   ADS-00   CIAE-00   DODE-00   NSAE-00   NSCE-00
       SSO-00   ICAE-00   INRE-00   PM-05   H-01   INR-10   L-03
       PA-01   SP-02   SS-15   HA-05   IO-14   PC-01   OCS-06   SY-05
       SYE-00   DCT-02   /083 W
       ------------------------015901   101334Z /4

O 100943Z JUN 80
FM AMEMBASSY SEOUL
TO SECSTATE WASHDC IMMEDIATE 6939
INFO AMEMBASSY TOKYO
COMUSKOREA SEOUL KS//BJ-IS
CHJUSMAG SEOUL KS
SA CINCUNC KS

C _____ ECTION 01 OF 10 SEOUL 07402

E.O. 12065: RDS-4 6/10/90 (MONJO, JOHN C.) OR-M
TAGS: SHUM, PINS, KS
SUBJECT: INSIDER'S ACCOUNT OF KWANGJU RIOT

1. (C) ENTIRE TEXT.

2. THERE FOLLOWS AN ACCOUNT OF THE KWANGJU RIOTS COM-
PILED BY [   ] OF LONG ACQUAINTANCE
WITH THE AREA. HE WAS IN KWANGJU THROUGHOUT THE PERIOD
OF TROUBLE AND, [

                          ] THIS IS THE MOST BALANCED
RECORD AND ANALYSIS OF INCIDENT WE HAVE SEEN SO FAR.
WE HAVE SUBSTITUTED [

                              ] STILL.   B/ A9

END-USERS SHOULD HANDLE REPORT WITH CARE [

                                                    B/ A9

BEGIN QUOTE:

ABBREVIATED RETROSPECT OF THE "MAY EIGHTEENTH INCIDENT" AT
KWANGJU, KOREA.

BEFORE MAY 18TH:

IN THE SPRING OF 1980 IN KWANGJU THERE WAS A GREAT DEAL OF

CAMPUS UNREST WHICH WAS FOCUSED ON ISSUES WITHIN THE
VARIOUS INDIVIDUAL CAMPUSES. WHETHER OR NOT THERE WAS A
PSYCHOLOGICAL LINK OR ANY RELATIONSHIP, THIS ANTAGONIST
STANCE WITHIN THE INSTITUTIONS WAS FOLLOWED BY A REVIVAL
OF ANTI-GOVERNMENT ACTIVITY.

ON THURSDAY, MAY 15TH, STUDENTS HELD A LARGE ANTI-GOVERN-
MENT RALLY WITH SONGS, SLOGANS, MARCHING, AND IN THE EVEN-
ING A TORCHLIGHT PARADE, ALL DIRECTED AGAINST THE YUSIN
CONSTITUTION AND THE CONTINUED IMPOSITION OF MARTIAL LAW
IN KOREA. THE ROUTINE AIR-RAID DRILL HELD ON THE 15TH OF
EACH MONTH WAS CANCELLED THIS DAY. RIOT POLICE WERE OUT
IN FORCE IN KWANGJU BUT TOOK NO ACTION OF ANY SORT, SIMPLY
WATCHING PASSIVELY FROM THEIR POSITIONS.

ON FRIDAY, MAY 16TH, CERTAIN STREETS IN KWANGJU WERE
CORDONED OFF, AND RIOT POLICE WERE IN EVIDENCE. IN THE
EVENING THERE WAS A TORCHLIGHT PARADE AND SHOUTS AND SONGS
AGAINST MARTIAL LAW AND AGAINST CHUN TU HWAN BY NAME.
(ONE BILINGUAL HEARER IS CONVINCED THAT THE WORDS HE HEARD
TO THE CHRISTIAN PEP-SONG "I'VE GOT PEACE LIKE A RIVER",
ETC., WERE OTHER WORDS CHOSEN FOR THE PROTEST.) NO POLICE
ACTION APPEARS TO HAVE BEEN TAKEN. THE RALLY WAS OVER BY
ABOUT 9:00 O'CLOCK.

RELATED OR NOT, MISSIONARIES WISHING TO GO TO TAEJON FOUND
BUS TICKETS COMPLETELY UNAVAILABLE AND WERE TOLD THAT IT
WAS ON ACCOUNT OF SOLDIERS GOING TO TAEJON. GOING BY TRAIN
ON SATURDAY, THEY FOUND LARGE NUMBERS OF ENLISTED MEN ON
THE TRAIN, WHOSE BEHAVIOR GREW PROGRESSIVELY UNRULY TO THE
PHYSICAL DANGER OF CIVILIAN PASSENGERS AND THE SHEDDING OF
BLOOD AMONG THE TROOPS. NO OFFICERS WERE IN EVIDENCE.

SATURDAY IN KWANGJU WAS QUIET. ON SATURDAY, HOWEVER, THE
EXTENSION OF MARTIAL LAW AND THE CLOSING OF COLLEGES OF
MANY CATEGORIES WAS ANNOUNCED, TAKING EFFECT AT MIDNIGHT.
ON SUNDAY, MAY 18TH:

THE KWANGJU MISSIONARIES DO NOT KNOW HOW OR WHEN THINGS BE-
CAME VIOLENT ON SUNDAY, MAY 18. IN THE MORNING THINGS
APPEARED QUIET, BUT BEGINNING AT ABOUT NOON--RETURNING
FROM ONE CHURCH OR ANOTHER--SOME OF THE MISSIONARIES RAN
INTO INDICATIONS OF PREVIOUS TROUBLE. ONE MOTHER
AND CHILDREN, WITH GUEST AMERICANS,   B1 A9
SAW NO SIGN OF TROUBLE BUT WERE IN THE WAY OF A HEAVY DIS-
CHARGE OF TEAR GAS, WHICH WOULD HARDLY HAVE BEEN USED FOR
A WHIM. HER HUSBAND, IN ANOTHER LOCATION, FOUND STREETS
CLOSED WHICH HAD BEEN OPEN EARLIER, AND ALSO DETECTED SIGNS
OF TEAR GAS USED EARLIER. OTHER MISSIONARIES SAW NOTHING.

TEXT OF TELEGRAM 80SEOUL 007402

AT SOME TIME ON SUNDAY TROOPS OF AN AIRBORNE UNIT APPEARED
IN THE CITY. SOME SAY AT 9:00 A.M., OTHERS AT NOON.

ON SUNDAY AFTERNOON THERE BEGAN TO BE UNPROVOKED ASSAULTS
BY AIRBORNE UNIT PERSONNEL UPON YOUNG MEN. INCIDENTS WERE
PERSONALLY WITNESSED BY

WHATEVER PRIOR PROVOCATION THERE MAY HAVE BEEN, THESE
PEOPLE WITNESSED ATTACKS OF GREATER OR LESSER SEVERITY ON

NNN

TEXT OF TELEGRAM BOSEOUL 007402

ADP053
CONFIDENTIAL

INFO OCT-01 ADS-00 CIAE-00 DODE-00 NSAE-00 NSCE-00
      SSO-00 ICAE-00 INRE-00 PM-05 H-01 INR-10 L-03
      PA-01 SP-02 SS-15 HA-05 IO-14 PC-01 OCS-06 /076 W
      ------------------014982 101141Z /13

O 100943Z JUN 80
FM AMEMBASSY SEOUL
TO SECSTATE WASHDC IMMEDIATE 6940
INFO AMEMBASSY TOKYO
COMUSKOREA SEOUL KS//BJ-IS
CHJUSMAG SEOUL KS
SA CINCUNC KS

CONFIDENTIAL SECTION 02 OF 10 SEOUL 07402

A NUMBER OF YOUNG MEN SIMPLY WALKING DOWN THE STREETS.
(DETAILS CAN BE PROVIDED IF REQUIRED.)

AT NO TIME DURING THE ENTIRE MAY 18TH INCIDENT, EITHER ON
THAT DAY OR THE DAYS FOLLOWING, DID ANY MISSIONARY SEE OR
HEAR EVEN AT SECOND OR THIRD HAND ANY INDICATION OF BRU-
TALITY BY THE CIVILIAN RIOT POLICE. THE RIOT POLICE WERE
SEEN TO STAND AT THEIR POSTS WITHOUT INTERFERING WHILE
AIRBORNE UNIT TROOPS ATTACKED PEOPLE. THERE WAS LATER A
RUMOR THAT ONE KOREAN POLICEMAN HAD BEEN KILLED WHILE TRY-
ING TO INTERFERE WITH AN AIRBORNE UNIT TROOPER'S ATTACK
UPON A PERSON, BUT NO PROOF. [   ] SAW A
CONFLICT BETWEEN A TRAFFIC OFFICER AND AN AIRBORNE UNIT
SOLDIER AT AN INTERSECTION, WHERE THE SOLDIER WANTED A
YOUNG WOMAN (APPARENTLY) OUT OF A TAXICAB, AND THE OFFICER
WANTED HIM TO LET THE CAB GO ON. (THE MISSIONARY NEVER
SAW THE OUTCOME, AS HE HAD TO KEEP GOING HIMSELF. IT
COULD HAVE BEEN SCARE TACTICS AND NOT AN ASSAULT. AT THIS
TIME THERE WERE NO REPORTS OF ANY MOLESTATION OF WOMEN
STUDENTS; ONLY THIS INCIDENT SEEN BY [

B1 19

B1 A9

REPORTS ON MONDAY TOLD OF INCREASINGLY WIDESPREAD BRUTALITY
ON SUNDAY EVENING. IN THE LATE AFTERNOON OF SUNDAY THE
[   ] SAW "NORMAL BRUTALITY" WITH NIGHTSTICKS
AND KICKING OF FALLEN MEN (LOOKING FROM THE WINDOWS OF THE
KWANGJU TOURIST HOTEL).

B1 A9

A CURFEW WAS ANNOUNCED FOR 8:00 AT AFTER 6:30, BUT THEN
CHANGED TO 9:00.

TEXT OF TELEGRAM BOSEOUL 007402

IN ALL OF THIS, THE WRITER WENT TO THE COUNTRY IN THE MORN-
ING, BACK IN THE EARLY AFTERNOON, AND TO CHURCH IN THE CITY
IN THE EVENING--EARLY BECAUSE OF THE ANNOUNCED CURFEW--AND
NEITHER SAW NOR HEARD ANYTHING AMISS. IT IS A MATTER OF
ROUTES AND LOCATIONS.

ON MONDAY, MAY 19TH:

MOST OF THE ACCOUNTS OF BRUTALITY COME FROM MONDAY, AL-
THOUGH THERE IS NO DOUBT THAT SUNDAY HAD ITS SHARE.

THE WRITER S FAMILY SEEMS SINGULARLY EXEMPT FROM TROUBLE-
SOME MATTERS, EVEN AT SECOND HAND.

(FULLER NOTES, NOT HERE COPIED, GIVE
DETAILS AND SOURCES.)

B/ A9

REPORTS OF SEVERE VIOLENCE BEGAN COMING IN ON MONDAY MORN-
ING. PERHAPS BY COINCIDENCE, THE FIRST REPORTED RIOT-TYPE
ACTIVITY WAS REPORTED ON MONDAY AFTERNOON, WHEN MR. DAVID
MILLER OF THE USIS TELEPHONED AND SAID THERE HAVE BEEN AN
ATTEMPT (ATTEMPTS?) TO SET FIRE TO GOVERNMENT BUILDINGS.

SMALL-SCALE RESISTANCE, IF IT CAN BE CALLED THAT, WAS SEEN

FROM THE FIRST.   PERSONAL
VIEWING OF AN ATTACK WAS ON SUNDAY AFTERNOON WHEN THREE
SOLDIERS JOINED IN BEATING A PASSERBY, AND PEOPLE THREW
STONES AT THEM, WITH THE RESULT THAT TWO RAN AFTER THE
STONE-THROWERS (WITHOUT SUCCESS) AND THE THIRD CONTINUED
BEATING THE YOUNG MAN. THERE WAS ALSO STONE-THROWING ON
MONDAY.

B/ A9

MONDAY WAS THE FIRST DAY WHEN WE HEARD REPORTS OF AIRBORNE
UNIT SOLDIERS ENTERING HOUSES IN SEARCH OF YOUNG MEN. CITY
BUSES WERE STOPPED AND YOUNG MEN TAKEN OFF AND BEATEN;
PUBLIC BUILDINGS AND EATING PLACES WERE GIVEN THE SAME
TREATMENT. IT IS NOT CERTAIN WHETHER PRIVATE HOMES WERE
ENTERED OR NOT. (KWANGJU CITIZENS SAY THEY WERE, BUT WE
HAVE NOT HEARD OF SPECIFIC CASES.)

A KOREAN PASTOR, WHO CAN BE NAMED IF NECESSARY, HEARD THE
AIRBORNE UNIT PERSONNEL SPEAKING WITH A DISTINCTIVELY
KYONGSANG ACCENT, AND REPORTS HEARING THEM SAY THEY WERE
GOING TO SLAY THE NO-GOOD CHOLLA-DO RASCALS. ANOTHER WIT-
NESS SAW OTHER AIRBORNE UNIT TROOPS BEHAVING WITH A BREAK-
DOWN OF DISCIPLINE SIMILAR TO WHAT TOOK PLACE WITH OTHER
TROOPS ON THE TRAIN TO TAEJON ON SATURDAY, AND NOTICED
THAT THE MEN PRESUMABLY GUARDING THE CHOSUN UNIVERSITY
LOOKED DISHEVELED, WERE OBVIOUSLY DRUNK, AND WERE SHOUTING
FOR FOOD. (THERE IS A RUMOR CURRENT THAT THE MEN WERE IN-

TEXT OF TELEGRAM 80SEOUL 007402

TENTIONALLY UNDERFED--AND SOME ADD. GIVEN DRINK; AND OTHERS
ADD. GIVEN DRUGS--TO MAKE THEM WILD.)

REPORTS OR RUMORS OF GIRLS STRIPPED TO THEIR UNDERCLOTHES
HAVE TURNED OUT TO BE NOT FROM THE SOURCES TO WHICH THEY
WERE ATTRIBUTED. AND SO FAR HAVE NOT BEEN VERIFIED BY ANY-

NNN

TEXT OF TELEGRAM 80SEOUL 007402

ADROS4
C

INFO   OCT-01 ADS-00 CIAE-00 DODE-00 NSAE-00 NSCE-00
       SSO-00 ICAE-00 INRE-00 PM-05 H-01 INR-10 L-03
       PA-01 SP-02 SS-15 HA-05 IO-14 PC-01 OCS-06 /076 W
       ------------------015005 1011412 /13
O 100943Z JUN 80
FM AMEMBASSY SEOUL
TO SECSTATE WASHDC IMMEDIATE 6941
INFO AMEMBASSY TOKYO
COMUSKOREA SEOUL KS//BJ-IS
CHJUSMAG SEOUL KS
SA CINCUNC KS

C   A L SZETION 03 OF 10 SEOUL 07402

BODY WHOM WE HAVE FOUND.

BOTH THE YWCA AND THE CATHOLIC CENTER WERE ENTERED AND
SEARCHED WITH A DEGREE OF VIOLENCE BETTER CALCULATED TO
COW THAN TO FLUSH OUT PEOPLE IN HIDING.

ON MONDAY AFTERNOON AN   ] B1A9
SAW YOUNG MEN ROUNDED UP AND TAKEN OFF, AND WITNESSED RE-
PEATED ASSAULTS ON SOME OF THE YOUNG MEN ALREADY APPRE-
HENDED.

MORE STONE-THROWING OCCURRED ON MONDAY; AND ON MONDAY MORN-
ING A[   ]SAW ACTUAL CIVILIAN INTERVENTION   B1 A9
ON BEHALF OF A PERSON UNDER ATTACK. (THIS WAS WHAT LOOKED
LIKE A MOTHER, YOUNGER SISTER AND SMALLER CHILD WHEN--ONE
GUESSES--THE YOUNG MAN IN THEIR FAMILY WAS BEING HURT.)

PEACE CORPS VOLUNTEERS WON A GOOD NAMEGEOR AMERICANS AT
THIS TIME BY A SORT OF NON-VIOLENT INTERVENTION. A PCV
SEEING A PERSON BEING BEATEN WOULD GO AND PUT THEIR ARMS
AROUND THE PERSON, THUS BEING IN THE WAY OF FURTHER BEAT-

ING. ON SUCH AN OCCASION THE ATTACKER WOULD LEAVE HIS
VICTIM BUT CHOOSE ANOTHER, WHO IN HIS TURN WOULD BE PRO-
TECTED BY A PCV WHO PUT HIS ARMS AROUND HIM.

IT IS THE SPONTANEOUS AND UNANIMOUS OPINION OF THE
MISSIONARY COMMUNITY LIVING TOGETHER HERE THAT THE PEACE
CORPS VOLUNTEERS HAVE WON THE LASTING GRATITUDE OF GREAT
NUMBERS OF THE CITIZENS OF KWANGJU FOR THE UNITED STATES.
SHARING THE LIFE OF THE PEOPLE WHOM THEY CAME TO SERVE.

TEXT OF TELEGRAM 80SEOUL 007402

EVEN WHEN IT MEANT SHARING SERIOUS, PERHAPS MORTAL, DANGER,
THEY MADE EVERYBODY WHO SAW THEM REALIZE THAT AMERICANS
(AND AMERICA) REALLY CARE. THEY IDENTIFIED THEMSELVES WITH
THE PEOPLE NOTSOY SHARED ANIMOSITIES BUT BY SHARED TROUBLE.
MISSIONARIES STAY AS A MATTER OF COURSE, IN OBEDIENCE TO A
MASTER AND IN A BOND OF LOVE WHICH LEAVES NO CHOICE; BUT
THE PEACE CORPS VOLUNTEERS WERE, IC ANYTHING, DISOBEDIENT
TO THEIR OWN MASTER IN NOT LEAVING THE CITY. IT IS MY
PERSONAL OPINION THAT IF THEIR HEADQUARTERS HAD BEEN ABLE
TO SEE THE SITUATION FROM THE GROUND AS WE SAW IT, HEAD-
QUARTERS WOULD HAVE HOPED THAT THEY WOULD STAY AND DO AL-
MOST EXACTLY WHAT THEY DID. AS AMERICANS, WE ARE VERY
PROUD OF OUR PEACE CORPS FRIENDS.

WE HEARD OF NO VIOLENT OR RIOT-TYPE DEMONSTRATIONS BEFORE
REPORTS OF AIRBORNE UNIT TROOPS' ATTACKS UPON STUDENTS.
WE HEARD OF NO NON-VIOLENT DEMONSTRATIONS AFTER THE REPORTS
BEGAN TO CIRCULTE. AGAIN, WE HEARD OF NO VIOLENT OR RIOT-
TYPE ACTIVITIES AFTER THE WITHDRAWAL OF THE FORCES OF LAW
AND ORDER FROM THE CITY. WE ASSUME THAT THERE WILL HAVE
BEEN TH)EVERY AND PERSONAL VIOLENCE, BUT WE HAVE NO DATA
TO SUPPORT OUR ASSUMPTION. THERE WAS DEFINITELY ABSOLUTELY
NO LOOTING, AND NO WANTON DAMAGE SUCH AS IS ASSOCIATED WITH
(FOR INSTANCE) MIAMI OR AMERICAN URBAN RIOTS, EXCEPT DURING

THE TIME WHEN TROOPS WERE TRYING TO PUT DOWN THE DEMONSTRA-
TIONS. THIS VIOLENCE BEGAN ON MONDAY AND CONTINUED UNTIL
THE TROOPS (AND WITH THEM THE POLICE) WERE WITHDRAWN FROM
THE CITY.

ON MONDAY CARS AND BUSES WERE BURNED.

WE RE NOT SURE WHEN THE CITIZENRY JOINED THE STUDENTS.
IT MAY HAVE BEEN ON MONDAY NIGHT. IT WAS CERTAINLY NO
LATER THAN TUESDAY.

WE DO NOT KNOW WHO TOLD WHAT TO WHOM, BUT THE AIRBORNE UNIT
TROOPS DID NOT REMAIN IN KWANGJU CITY AFTER MONDAY, SO FAR
AS WE CAN TELL. THE APPEARANCE IS THAT THEY WERE PULLED
OUT BY OR AT ABOUT MIDNIGHT ON MONDAY, AND REPLACED (BY
TROOPS FROM NORTH CHOLLA?).

ON TUESDAY, MAY 20TH:

ON TUESDAY MORNING THERE WERE APPARENTLY NO TROOPS IN
KWANGJU OF THE AIRBORNE UNIT, THEIR PLACE HAVING BEEN
TAKEN BY "NORTH CHOLLA" TROOPS. (SOME DAYS LATER
     WE KNOW, IN THE CITY--NOT IN UNIFORM OF COURSE--
STUMBLED ON TWO AIRBORNE UNIT MEN VERY UNKEMPT AND APPAR-
ENTLY LOST AND FRIGHTENED. HE HAD A SCUFFLE WITH THEM AND
CAME OUT AHEAD. THIS SEEMS TO BE SIMPLY TWO MEN WHO GOT

B / A9

TEXT OF TELEGRAM 80SEOUL 007402

SEPARATED FROM THEIR OUTFIT AND LEFT BEHIND IN A HOSTILE
CITY.)

TUESDAY MORNING WAS QUIET. A   WENT
TO THE BANK AND GOT SOME MONEY. SAW YOUNG PEOPLE OF THE
"VICTIM" AGE GROUP WALKING UNCONCERNED.

NNN

TEXT OF TELEGRAM 80SEOUL 007402

ADP636

INFO OCT-01 ADS-00 CIAE-00 DODE-00 NSAE-00 NSCE-00
      SSO-00 ICAE-00 INRE-00 PM-05 H-01 INR-10 L-03
      NSC-05 PA-01 SP-02 SS-15 ICA-11 HA-05 IO-14 PC-01
      OES-09 SY-05 SYE-00 DCT-02 /102 W
                  ------------------022480 110738Z /13/43
O 100943Z JUN 80
FM AMEMBASSY SEOUL
TO SECSTATE WASHDC IMMEDIATE 6942
INFO AMEMBASSY TOKYO
COMUSKOREA SEOUL KS//BJ-IS
CHJUSMAG SEOUL KS
SA CINCUNC KS

L SECTION 04 OF 10 SEOUL 07402

C O R R E C T E D C O P Y (TEXT)

RUMORS SPREAD ON TUESDAY THAT THE HOUSE-SEARCHES OF MONDAY
NIGHT WERE A PRELUDE TO PLANNED EXTENSIVE HOUSE-TO-HOUSE
SEARCH-AND ABDUCTION PLANS FOR TUESDAY NIGHT. WE ASSUME
THESE RUMORS TO BE BASELESS, BUT THEY WERE BELIEVED. ALSO
BELIEVED WERE STORIES OF AIRBORNE UNIT MEN WAVING SEVERED
BREASTS ON THEIR BAYONETS. WE HAVE BEEN HARD PUT TO FIND
SUBSTANTIATED STORIES OF WORSE TREATMENT OF WOMEN THAN OF
MEN, AND MOST OF THE SPECIFIC STORIES WE HAVE HEARD CON-
CERNED NOT WOMEN BUT MEN. HOW TRUE THE RUMORS ARE LIKELY
TO BE IS A MATTER ON WHICH OUR MISSIONARY GROUP IS NOT IN
FULL AGREEMENT.

A LARGE RALLY ON TUESDAY NIGHT RAN LATE IN DEFIANCE OF THE
9:00 CURFEW. ON TUESDAY NIGHT WE HEARD A MODERATELY LARGE
AMOUNT OF GUNFIRE, AND ON WEDNESDAY MORNING WE DISCOVERED
THE TROOPS AND POLICE APPARENTLY GONE FROM KWANGJU.

A MARTIAL LAW COMMAND LEAFLET (OF WEDNESDAY, MAY 21) SAYS

THAT ON TUESDAY NIGHT THE TROOPS AND POLICE SUFFERED TEN
CASUALTIES (KILLED OR WOUNDED), AND THAT PUBLIC BUILDINGS,
POLICE STATION AND THREE BROADCAST STATIONS HAD BEEN DES-
TROYED OR BURNED.

NOT ALL TROOPS HAD LEFT THE CITY ON TUESDAY, NONETHELESS
AND THERE WAS MORE FIGHTING ON WEDNESDAY.

A PAPER WRITTEN BY A KOREAN ENGLISH TEACHER AND ADDRESSED

TEXT OF TELEGRAM 80SEOUL 007402

TO A FOREIGN CORRESPONDENT SAYS THAT THE "MBC" TELEVISION
STATION CAUGHT FIRE BY ACCIDENT AND THAT STUDENTS TRIED IN
VAIN TO SAVE IT. WE HAVE NO CONFIRMATION.

RUMOR HAS IT THAT THE SOCALLED "V.O.C.", THE STATIONOF A
LOCAL NEWSPAPER, WAS DESTROYED BY TROOPS. WE HAVENO CON-
FORMATION.

ON WEDNESDAY, MAY 21ST:

THERE WAS FIGHTING ON WEDNESDAY, BUT NONE OF US SAW IT, AL-
THOUGH WE DID HEAR GUNFIRE AND SEE SMOKE. [
                    ]DROVE SOME PEOPLE TO THE COUNTRY AND RETURNED,
BUT WHILE HE SAW BURNING VEHICLES AND HAD SOME ENCOUNTERS
WITH THE MILITANT CITIZENRY, HE SAW NO SECTION OF THE CITY
(WHERE HIS ROAD TOOK HIM; OR LATER WHERE HE WENT FOR PHOTO-
GRAPHS) WHICH HAD EITHER TROOPS OR POLICE IN EVIDENCE.

WEDNESDAY MORNING WAS SURPRISING, NOT SIMPLY BECAUSE THE
POLICE AND TROOPS WERE QANESROM OUR SIGHT, BUT BECAUSE WE
SAW UNMISTAKABLY THAT ALL VISIBLE CITIZENRY APPLAUDED THE
STUDENTS, AND THAT--BARRING ANY UNKNOWN AND DISCREETLY
SILENT CITIZENS--THE ENTIRE CITY HAD EMBRACED AND ADOPTED
THE STUDENT PROTEST.

PAGE 03   SEOUL 07402   04 OF 10   110732Z

FROM THIS POINT ON, THE MAY EIGHTEENTH INCIDENT WAS CLEARLY
A MATTER OF THE CITIZENRY OF KWANGJU, AND SHOULD NOT BE
SPOKEN OF IN TERMS OF STUDENTS. I WAS MYSELF ONE OF THE
SLOWEST TO RECOGNIZE THIS FACT, BUT I WAS FORCED TO IT AND
I CONSIDER IT BEYOND DEBATE.

-   EDITORIAL PARAGRAPH; MAY BE SKIPPED:

-   IN MY OWN OPINION, WHAT WE SAW IN KWANGJU WAS A DEMON-
-   STRATION OF FREE PEOPLE PUSHED TOO FAR, AND REACTING
-   WITH VIOLENT INDIGNATION WHICH IS DIVORCED FROM POLICY
-   OR PLAN AND WHICH INSPIRES A TEMPORARY LAWLESSNESS IN
-   LAW-ABIDING PEOPLE. I LIKEN IT TO THE BOSTON TEA
-   PARTY; LAWLESS, EMOTIONAL, DUYTRUCTIVE AND ILL-CALCU-
-   LATED FOR THE ACHIEVEMENT OF BENEFIT; SPONTANEOUS COM-
-   BUSTION WHEN FREEBORN CITIZENS SUDDENLY REFUSED TO BE
-   TROMPED UPON ANY LONGER. THIS OPINION IS REINFORCED
-   BY THE MANNER IN WHICH THE CITY HANDLES ITS RETURN TO
-   SANITY, WHICH COMES VERY SOON NOW.

ON WEDNESDAY MORNING YOUNG MEN AND WOMEN CAREENED THROUGH
THE STREETS ON COMANDEERED PICK-UPS, BUSES, AND MILITARY-
TYPE ARMY OR POLICE VEHICLES, WITH SLOGANS PAINTED ON THEM.
AS THEY WENT BY, YOUNG AND OLDER SOBER CITIZENS STOOD BY
THE STREETS APPLAUDING AND CHEERING. TWICE I SAW WOMEN

TEXT OF TELEGRAM BOSEOUL 007402

RUN OUT WITH BUNDLES OF STICKS OR CUDGELS FOR THE STUDENTS.
LATER THE OFFERINGS WERE SOFT DRINKS AND BUNS (NEVER DID I
SEE LIQUOR GIVEN, OR STUDENTS DRUNK).
THE MOOD OF STUDENTS AND CITIZENRY WAS HEADY AND EXHILA-
RATED, AND ORDINARY RULES WERE CLEARLY IN ABEYANCE. A VERY
FEW RIFLES WERE IN EVIDENCE, BUT THE MOOD WAS LESS LIKE THE
EVE OF BATTLE THAN LIKE THE NIGHT BEFORE THE HOMETOWN
TEAM'S GAME OF THE SEASON.

NNN

TEXT OF TELEGRAM BOSEOUL 007402

INFO OCT-01 ADS-00 CIAE-00 DODE-00 NSAE-00 NSCE-00
      SSO-00 ICAE-00 INRE-00 PM-05 H-01 INR-10 L-03
      PA-01 SP-02 SS-15 HA-05 IO-14 PC-01 OCS-06 /076 W
      ------------------015095 101140Z /13
O.100913Z PIN 80
FM AMEMBASSY SEOUL
TO SECSTATE WASHDC IMMEDIATE 6943
INFO AMEMBASSY TOKYO
COMUSKOREA SEOUL KS//BJ-IS
CHJUSMAG SEOUL KS
SA CINCUNC KS

C██████████████ L SECTION 05 OF 10 SEOUL 07402

SOMEWHERE, HOWEVER, THERE WAS FIGHTING. AT ABOUT NOON THE
[   ] SAW SMOKE AND WENT TO A POINT
FROM WHICH THEY COULD PLACE IT. THEY ARE SURE THAT THIS
WAS THE BURNING OF THE TAX OFFICE, ALTHOUGH ITS LOCATION
DID NOT SEEM TO HAVE BEEN HELD EARLIER IN THE DAY BY TROOPS
OR POLICE. IF IT WAS WANTONLY BURNED, AS CONTRASTED TO
BEING BURNED IN CONFLICT, IT IS OUR ONLY DEFINITE INSTANCE
OF RIOT-ACTIVITY THIS LATE. IN ANY CASE, THE BUILDING WAS
GUTTED, TOGETHER WITH AN ASSOCIATED BUILDING IN THE SAME
GROUNDS--AND WITH THE HOME AND RESTAURANT OF [
                    ] WHO LIVED TOO CLOSE TO ES-
CAPE THE FIRE.

B/19

A LITTLE BEFORE THIS [   ] ON THE LAST
JAUNT HE RISKED BY CAR, WAS TOLD OF "MANY BODIES" IN FRONT
OF THE CATHOLIC CENTER AND ASKED TO GO PHOTOGRAPH THEM,
BUT WAS UNABLE TO GET THERE BY CAR AND UNWILLING TO LEAVE
HIS CAR UNTENDED. HE FOUND PEOPLE NOT UNFRIENDLY TO HIM,
BUT IN A VERY ANGRY MOOD AT THIS POINT. [
          ] HOWEVER, DID SEE THESE DEAD.)

B/19

B/19

B/19

CASUALTIES BEGAN COMING IN AT NOON ON WEDNESDAY. ANY
EARLIER CASUALTIES ARE FOR THE MOST PART UNACCOUNTED FOR
EVEN AFTER THE CITY HAS BEEN REOCCUPIED AND THE DEAD
BURIED.

MANY CASUALTIES WERE NEEDLESS TRAGEDIES. WE HAVE A NUMBER
OF STORIES OF THESE. WE HAVE NO (OR ALMOST NO) INDICATION,
HOWEVER, OF WANTON CRUELTY AFTER THE WITHDRAWAL OF THE AIR-
BORNE UNIT TROOPS. THIS COULD BE BECAUSE OF THE CHANGE OF

TEXT OF TELEGRAM BOSEOUL 007402

TROOPS OR IT COULD BE BECAUSE A RIOT-CONTROL TYPE SITUA-
TION WAS SUCCEEDED BY AN ARMED-CONFLICT TYPE SITUATION.
(THE FIRST CASUALTY IN THE KWANGJU CHRISTIAN HOSPITAL WAS
A MAN BAYONETTED IN THE BACK WHILE TRYING TO FIND OUT
ABOUT ONE OR MORE OF HIS CHILDREN, BUT THE CIRCUMSTANCES
MAKE IT UNCLEAR WHETHER THE SOLDIER KNEW HIM TO BE INNO-
CENT. IF HE WAS WOUNDED AT NOON IN THE NEIGHBORHOOD OF
THE TOURIST HOTEL, AS REPORTED, ANY SOLDIERS THERE AT THAT
TIME WILL HAVE BEEN FACING AN EXTREMELY HOSTILE AND
DANGEROUS CROWD.)
CROWDS WERE WARNED TO DISPERSE OR BE FIRED ON BY HELICOP-
TERS, BUT THERE WAS GREAT INDIGNATION WHEN FIRING ACTUALLY
TOOK PLACE.

FROM 3:00 TO 4:00 ON WEDNESDAY AFTERNOON THERE WAS A SPATE
OF CASUALTIES, BOTH DEAD AND WOUNDED--TEN DEAD AND FIFTY
WOUNDED BY ABOUT 4:00 IN THE KWANGJU CHRISTIAN HOSPITAL
(BUT BY THURSDAY NOON THE DEAD BROUGHT THERE TOTALED ONLY
13 OR 15, ALTHOUGH THERE WERE MORE WOUNDED).

ON WEDNESDAY NIGHT MANY PEOPLE CAME TO THE COMPOUND IN THE
HOPE OF SAFETY FROM SUPPOSED HOUSE-TO-HOUSE SEARCH-AND-
SEIZURE OR OTHER DANGERS. MOSTLY THEY WERE PEOPLE'S SONS,
BUT THERE WERE OTHERS ALSO. NONE STAYED AT MY HOUSE.

81 A9

WEDNESDAY DARKNESS BROUGHT A LARGE INCREASE IN GUNFIRE,
MUCH OF IT SEEMING TO BE IN THE IMMEDIATE VICINITY.

THE LATTER PART OF THE NIGHT WAS MUCH MORE QUIET, DESPITE
A SUPPOSEDLY SURE WORD THAT THE CITY WAS TO BE REOCCUPIED
DURING WEDNESDAY NIGHT.

ON THURSDAY, MAY 22ND:

81 A9

TEXT OF TELEGRAM BOSEOUL 007402

B/ 19

NNN

TEXT OF TELEGRAM BOSEOUL 007402

ADP051
~~CONFIDENTIAL~~

INFO   OCT-01   ADS-00   CIAE-00   DODE-00   NSAE-00   NSCE-00
       SSO-00   ICAE-00   INRE-00   PM-05   H-01   INR-10   L-03
       PA-01   SP-02   SS-15   HA-05   IO-14   PC-01   OCS-06   /076 W
       ------------------015175   101140Z /11

O 100943Z JUN 80
FM AMEMBASSY SEOUL
TO SECSTATE WASHDC IMMEDIATE 6944
INFO AMEMBASSY TOKYO
COMUSKOREA SEOUL KS//BJ-IS
CHJUSMAG SEOUL KS
SA CINCUNC KS

~~CONFIDENTIA~~ L SECTION 06 OF 10 SEOUL 07402

B/ A9

IN TWO CARS WITH AMERICAN FLAGS AND "FOREIGNER'S CAR"
SIGNS, THEY MADE A CIRCUITOUS TRIP TO SONGJONGNI, CONVOYED
PART WAY BY CITIZENRY. SONGJONGNI ALSO BEING IN CITIZENS'
HANDS, AND NO TRAINS RUNNING, THEY RETURNED AND TOOK THE
EXPRESS HIGHWAY NORTH UNTIL TURNED BACK BY A MILITARY
GUARD ON THE HIGHWAY. THE SOLDIERS SAID, HOWEVER, THAT
TRAINS WERE SERVING A STATION WITHIN REACH A LITTLE BACK
ON THE ROAD   THIS PROVED TRUE. AND AFTER SEEING THE PARTY
OFF, THE TWO CARS RETURNED TO KWANGJU. ENROUTE THEY WERE
STOPPED AT A NEWLY ERECTED BARRICADE AND TOLD THAT THE CITY
WAS UNDER ATTACK. THIS WAS NOT STRICTLY ACCURATE, AS THEY
FOUND OUT WHEN FINALLY ALLOWED TO GO ON. MET BY CITIZENRY
AT THE EDGE OF THE CITY, THEY WERE CONVOYED MOST OF THE
WAY HOME BY DIFFERENT STREETS THAN BEFORE, AND ARRIVED
WITHOUT INCIDENT.

(CITIZENRY FAITHFULLY SUPPLIED THOSE IN VEHICLES WITH FOOD
AND DRINK. ON THIS TRIP BACK TO KWANGJU.
         WAS TOSSED A BUN FROM CITIZENRY IN A COMMAN-   B/ A9
DEERED BUS, BUT WITH TOO POOR AN AIM, AND PROCEEDED
BUNLESS.)

TWO RUMORS ROSE FROM THIS EXCURSION: ONE, THAT THE MISSION-
ARIES HAD ALL LEFT THE CITY, AND ONE THAT AMERICAN EMBASSY
STAFF HAD ENTERED KWANGJU WITH FLAGS FLYING. SO WE DO NOT

FEEL WE WOULD BE JUSTIFIED IN RELYING HEAVILY ON OTHER
RUMORS WHICH WE HEAR.

RUMORS AGAIN CONFIDENTLY FORETOLD THE OCCUPATION OF THE
CITY ON THURSDAY NIGHT.   FROM 11:00 P.M. UNTIL 12:30 THE
WRITER'S FAMILY ⟦ ⟧ HEARD SUSTAINED AND HEAVY FIRING INCLUDING
WEAPONRY LARGER THAN SMALL ARMS.   THERE WAS A DISCERNIBLE
PROGRESSION FROM THE VICINITY OF THE MILITARY UNIT HALF-
WAY TO SONGJONGNI IN THE WEST, IN A SOUTHWARD ARC AND
AROUND TO A POINT SOUNDING IN THE NIGHT LIKE THE NEIGHBOR-
HOOD OF THE PROVINCIAL CAPITOL.
IN THE MORNING THERE WAS NO SIGN OF ANY SUCH ACTION HAVING
TAKEN PLACE, SO FAR AS OBSERVATIONS POSSIBLE TO US REVEALED.

FRIDAY THROUGH MONDAY, MAY 23RD THROUGH 26TH:

THE NEXT FOUR DAYS, FRIDAY, SATURDAY, SUNDAY AND MONDAY,
WERE A TIME OF NEGOTIATION AND MUTUAL FOREBEARANCE BY MILI-
TARY AND CITIZENRY IN THE EFFORT TO RESTORE REGULAR GOVERN-
MENT TO KWANGJU.

IN THIS THE INITIATIVE SEEMS TO HAVE BEEN TAKEN BY THE
CHRISTIAN CLERGY.   WE RECOGNIZE THAT THE COINCIDENCE IS SO

PERFECT AS TO MAKE OUR ACCOUNT SUSPECT, BUT THE FACT RE-
MAINS THAT THE MAJOR ROLE SEEMS TO HAVE BEEN PLAYED BY
PASTORS OF THE TWO KOREAN DENOMINATIONS WITH WHICH WE ARE
MOST CLOSELY ASSOCIATED ⟧

B/ A9

B/ A9

FOUR TIMES, ACCORDING TO ⟦   ⟧   THE
MILITARY CONSENTED TO POSTPONE MILITARY ACTION AT THE PLEA
OF THE RECONCILIATION COMMITTEE (RECONCILIATION; RESOLU-
TION; SETTLEMENT.   SETTLEMENT PROCEDURE COMMITTEE? --
SOO-SUP TAE-CHAEK COMMITTEE).

B/ A9

MEANWHILE THERE WAS NO NIGHT WHEN FIRING DID NOT OCCUR.
TROOPS ADVANCED WELL INTO THE CITY AND WITHDREW.   ON AT
LEAST ONE OCCASION THEY WITHDREW WHEN A DELEGATION OF
PASTORS WENT AND ASKED THEM TO ON THE GROUNDS THAT THEY
HAD AGREED NOT TO COME YET INTO THE CITY.

ON FRIDAY MORNING THE ⟦   ⟧
⟦ ⟧ FAMILY SAW TWO UNIFORMED SOLDIERS WALKING THROUGH
OUR OWN HILL, BUT DID NOT SPEAK TO THEM OR THEY TO HIM.

B/ A9

MEANWHILE THE CITIZENRY MAINTAINED GOOD ORDER IN THE CITY.

TEXT OF TELEGRAM BOSEOUL 007402

AND BEGAN COLLECTING WEAPONS AND EXPLOSIVES TO AVOID
TROUBLE WHEN THE CITY WAS REOCCUPIED. (SOME PERHAPS AL-
READY FELT THAT THE COLLECTION WOULD ON THE CONTRARY PRO-
VIDE A DEPOT OF ARMS TO USE IN RESISTING REOCCUPATION, BUT
IF SO IT WAS A PRIVATE OPINION.)
                    TOOK A LEAD IN SEEKING THE FORMATION OF AN

NNN

TEXT OF TELEGRAM 80SEOUL 007402

ADP260

CONFIDENTIAL

INFO   OCT-01 ADS-00 CIAE-00 DODE-00 NSAE-00 NSCE-00
       SSO-00 ICAE-00 INRE-00 PM-05 H-01 INR-10 L-03
       PA-01 SP-02 SS-15 HA-05 IO-14 PC-01 OCS-06 SY-05
       SYE-00 DCT-02 /083 W
       ------------------015219 101340Z /43
O 100943Z JUN 80
FM AMEMBASSY SEOUL
TO SECSTATE WASHDC IMMEDIATE 6946 .
INFO AMEMBASSY TOKYO
COMUSKOREA SEOUL KS//BJ-IS
CHJUSMAG SEOUL KS
SA CINCUNC KS

C O N F I D E N T I A L SECTION 08 OF 10 SEOUL 07402

BY AND LARGE THE HARD-LINE STUDENTS DID NOT REFUSE TO
ACCEPT THE SETTLEMENT ACHIEVED, BUT SOME OF THEM FELT WITH
THE SOCIAL-ACTIVIST NEWCOMERS ON THE CONCERNED CITIZENS'
COMMITTEE THAT A LITTLE TOUGHER BARGAINING WOULD BE BETTER.
THE SUICIDE GROUP OF COURSE WAS THE MAJOR PROBLEM.

WITH THE BREAKING OF THE CONSENSUS, THE DELEGATION COULD NO
LONGER SPEAK FOR THE CITY IN DEALING WITH THE MARTIAL LAW
COMMAND.

ON SUNDAY NIGHT WE RECEIVED A MESSAGE INDICATING THAT ONLY
MILITARY SECURITY FORBADE TELLING US OUTRIGHT THAT MILITARY
ACTION WOULD BEGIN ON SUNDAY NIGHT OR MONDAY. SINCE THERE
HAD BEEN NO NOTICE GIVEN THE CITY, WE THOUGHT THIS A BREAK-
ING OF A PROMISE, AND THEN
        AGREED TO SEEK MEMBERS OF THE RECONCILIATION DELEGA-
TION AND SUGGESTED THAT THEY ASK ENOUGH DELAY TO KEEP THE
PROMISE MADE BEFORE.

ON MONDAY MORNING THIS WAS CONFIRMED BY TROOP MOVEMENTS.

AND WE SET OUT ON THIS ERRAND; AND SAW POSTED ON THE
STREET NEW POSTERS OF AN INFLAMATORY NATURE, OVER A NAME
ALMOST BUT NOT EXACTLY LIKE THAT USED BY THE RECONCILIATION
PROCEDURES COMMITTEE. THE COMMITTEE MEMBER, WHOM THE
WRITER APPROACHED, SEEMED TO THE WRITER TO HAVE FELT THAT
HE HAD DONE ALL HE COULD DO, AND THAT THE BREAKING OF THE
CONSENSUS HAD RESULTED IN THE BREAKING OF THE CITY'S SIDE
OF THE ACHIEVED SETTLEMENT, SO THAT THE PROMISES WERE AL-
READY VOID. THE FABRICATED POSTERS WERE CLEARLY THE WORK

OF OTHERS. AND WOULD NOT BE BELIEVED BY INTELLIGENT PEOPLE.
CONTACT WAS OUT OF TOUCH AT THE
MOMENT. BUT WE MET SOME OTHERS, AND WERE TAKEN BY THEM TO
THE MEETING OF THE CONCERNED CITIZENS, NOT TO SPEAK BUT TO
LISTEN.

THERE HAD BEEN A DEADLINE ANNOUNCED, AND IN FACT THE MAR-
TIAL LAW TROOPS DID NOT COME UNTIL AFTER THAT DEADLINE
PASSED. SO EITHER OUR INTERPRETATION OF THE INFORMATION
WE RECEIVED WAS WRONG OR SOMEBODY TOOK ACTION AFTER ALL.

THE OCCUPATION OF THE CITY CAME ON MONDAY NIGHT, OR MORE
PROPERLY IN THE EARLY HOURS OF TUESDAY MORNING, MAY 27TH.

THE MILITARY OPERATION WAS SWIFT AND NEAT. THE GUNFIRE WE
HEARD WAS FAR LESS THAN WE HAD HEARD ON THE THURSDAY WHEN
IT HAD BEEN SO NOISY.

WE THINK IT CLEAR THAT THE OCCUPATION OF THE CITY WAS AS
RELATIVELY BLOODLESS AS IT TURNED OUT BECAUSE IN FACT THE
CITY DID NOT OPPOSE IT. THE ONLY ACTUAL OPPOSITION, WE
BELIEVE, WAS FRONT THE SUICIDE GROUP AND SOME TRAGIC HIGH
SCHOOL CHILDREN WHO JOINED THEM.

THE DAYS FROM FRIDAY THROUGH MONDAY WERE ALSO THE PERIOD
DURING WHICH AMERICANS WERE INSTRUCTED TO LEAVE KWANGJU.
TIME MAGAZINE'S ACCOUNT THAT "SOME MISSIONARIES" WERE RE-
CEIVED AT THE AIR FORCE BASE IS TRUE IN THAT THE YOUNG
PEOPLE WHO CAME AS MISSIONARIES OF THE LATTER DAY SAINTS
DID (WE HEAR) LEAVE KWANGJU. WE KNOW OF NO OTHER.

OUR PRESENCE WAS CONSPICUOUSLY (WORD CHO-
SEN BY DESIGN) SATISFYING TO ALL WE MET. TO HAVE LEFT
WOULD HAVE BEEN IMPOSSIBLE TO US EACH. AND HAD WE FORCED
OURSELVES TO LEAVE, THERE WOULD, WE THINK, HAVE BEEN NO
MORE PLACE FOR US TO SERVE IN THIS COMMUNITY.

FROM TUESDAY, MAY 27TH, THROUGH WEDNESDAY, JUNE 4TH:

THE CITY WAS REOCCUPIED IN THE DAYBREAK HOURS OF TUESDAY,
MAY 27. THE RADIO WARNED EVERYONE TO STAY OFF THE STREETS
THAT DAY. NOT ALL OF US OBEYED THE ORDER, BUT NONE OF US
SUFFERED HURT OR THREAT OF HURT.

FOLLOW-UP OPERATIONS SEEMED LARGELY TO BE NOT RETALIATORY
BUT SIMPLY FOR THE REMOVAL OF THOSE WHO STILL REFUSED TO
TURN IN ARMS OR ACCEPT THE RETURN OF POLICE AND TROOPS.
SIX WERE FLUSHED OUT OF OUR OWN HILL, AND WERE TAKEN INTO
CUSTODY IN A SITUATION WHERE THEY COULD MORE EASILY HAVE

TEXT OF TELEGRAM 80SEOUL 007402

BEEN SHOT BY THE TROOPS INTO WHOSE ARMS THEY WERE SKILL-
FULLY HERDED.

WE WERE SHOCKED BY AN INCIDENT AT THE YWCA, IN WHICH BLOOD
WAS SHED AND LIVES WERE LOST. LATER WE LEARNED (FROM
SOURCES MORE LIKELY TO BE SYMPATHETIC THAN NOT TO THE
YWCA) THAT AT THE TIME OF THIS INCIDENT THERE WAS A PRAYER

NNN

ADR167

PAGE 01   SEOUL 07402   09 OF 10   101953Z
ACTION EA-12

INFO   OCT-01   ADS-00   CIAE-00   DODE-00   NSAE-00   NSCE-00
       SSO-00   ICAE-00   INRE-00   PM-05   H-01   INR-10   L-03
       PA-01   SP-02   SS-15   HA-05   IO-14   PC-01   OCS-06   SY-05
       SYE-00   DCT-02   /083 W
                    -----------------018519   102000Z /61/43
O 100943Z JUN 80
FM AMEMBASSY SEOUL
TO SECSTATE WASHDC IMMEDIATE 6947
INFO AMEMBASSY TOKYO
COMUSKOREA SEOUL KS//BJ-IS
CHJUSMAG SEOUL KS
SA CINCUNC KS

SECTION 09 OF 10 SEOUL 07402

C O R R E C T E D   C O P Y (TEXT PARA 3)

MEETING HELD IN THE YWCA LATE INTO THE NIGHT IN VIOLATION
OF THE CURFEW, AND THAT ALTHOUGH THE GIRLS AT THE PRAYER
MEETING SLIPPED SAFELY HOME, THE BOYS CHOSE TO REMAIN, AND
THAT IN SPITS OF ALL THE TURNING IN OF WEAPONS, THE BOYS
HAD GUNS WITH THEM.   FINALLY, WE LEARNED THAT THERE WERE
ONLY TWO DEATHS, ONE OF AN EMPLOYEE ON DUTY AND ONE OF ONE
OF THE BOYS.

THE MAY 13 INCIDENT WAS NOT COMMUNIST INSPIRED OR INFIL-
TRATED OR INFECTED.   THIS IS CLEAR FACT, BUT WE HEAR--NOT
SURPRISINGLY--THAT THE TROOPS WHICH REOCCUPIED THE CITY
WERE GIVEN TO UNDERSTAND THAT THEY WERE DEALING WITH A
COMMUNIST INSURRECTION.   IF JUDGMENT IS TO BE PASSED, WE
THINK THIS MISINFORMATION OF THE TROOPS EXTREMELY UNFOR-
TUNATE.   THE OTHER SIDE OF THE COIN IS THE RESTRAINT BY
WHICH SO FEW CASUALTIES OCCURRED, EVEN WHEN THE TROOPS
THOUGHT IT WAS COMMUNISTS THEY WERE FIGHTING.

PAGE 02   SEOUL 07402   09 OF 10   101953Z

FOR THE KNOWN DEAD, THE CITY PROVIDED BURIAL SPACE IN THE
SUBURBAN CITY CEMETERY, BUT FAMILIES DID NOT HAVE THE OP-
TION OF BURIALS ELSEWHERE.   TRUCKS TOOK COFFINS, FREE BUSES
TOOK MOURNERS.   CITY GRAVEDIGGERS PREPARED ROW ON ROW OF
OPEN GRAVES, AND AFTER INTERMENT HELPED FINISH AND SOD THE
MOUNDS.   WE ATTENDED OR SHARED THE FUNERAL OF A SEMINARY
STUDENT WHOM WE UNDERSTAND TO HAVE BEEN EXEMPLARY IN BE-
HAVIOR AND KILLED ALMOST BY ACCIDENT WHILE GUARDING EXPLO-
SIVES FROM FALLING INTO WRONG HANDS.   THE MULTIPLE SIMUL-

TEXT OF TELEGRAM BOSEOUL 007402

TANEOUS BURIALS WERE EXTREMELY TAXING TO OBSERVE.

AS THE MAY EIGHTEENTH INCIDENT FALLS FARTHER INTO THE BACK-
GROUND WE BEGIN TO FEEL WE SEE INCREASING DEGREES OF RETAL-
IATION. ONE SOURCE SYMPATHETIC TO THE CITIZENS SAYS THAT
THE CONTRACT WAS BROKEN BY THE CITY AND THE PROMISE ALREADY
VOID. IF THE PROMISE IS NOT VOID, THE APPEARANCE IS THAT
IT HAS BEEN SOMEWHAT BROKEN. IF THE PROMISE IS VOID IN-
DEED, THE WONDER IS THAT THERE REMAINS THIS MUCH GENTLE-
NESS.

IF AN ABBREVIATED ACCOUNT IS THIS LONG, CONSIDER HOW MUCH
REMAINS UNSAID, BUT ONE FINAL POINT I AM DETERMINED TO
MAKE. IT IS THIS.

IN MY LIFE I HAVE NEVER FELT SUCH WONDERING PRIDE IN MY
KOREAN FRIENDS AS I HAVE FELT IN THE DAYS OF THIS MAY
EIGHTEENTH INCIDENT. ALL I HAD SUPPOSED ABOUT THE CHARAC-
TERISTICS OF THE KOREAN PEOPLE WAS SURPASSED BY WHAT WAS TO
ME AN INCREDIBLE WILLINGNESS TO PAY ANY PRICE REQUIRED IF
BY PAYING IT THEY COULD ACHIEVE GOOD. I MEAN PARTICULARLY
THE RESTRAINT SHOWED BY THE MILITARY AFTER THE FIRST TRAGIC
DAYS WHICH SET EVERYTHING OFF, AND THE DISCIPLINE AND RE-
STRAINT SHOWED BY THE CITIZENRY AT A TIME WHEN THEY BE-

LIEVED THINGS FAR MORE OUTRAGEOUS THAN THE TRAGIC TRUTH.

IN NO WAY DIMINISHING THE CREDIT DUE TO OUR KOREAN
FRIENDS, FIRST PRAISE GOES TO GOD, WHO IN HIS GOOD WILL
SAW FIT THIS TIME TO ANSWER OUR PRAYERS WITH DAILY MIRA-
CLES WORKED IN THE HEARTS OF HUNDREDS WHO KNOW HIM AND
THOUSANDS WHO DO NOT. IF I HAVE ONE REGRET IT IS TO END
THIS REPORT WITH NO MORE PRAISE THAN THIS.
I WISH NOW TO EMPHASIZE SOME IMPORTANT POINTS TO BE REMEM-
BERED:

1) KWANGJU WAS NEVER A RIOT-TORN CITY. FOR UNDER 24 HOURS
RIOT-TYPE ACTIVITY TOOK PLACE IN SPECIFIC AND LIMITED LOCA-
TIONS ON ACCOUNT OF THE CITIZENS' OUTRAGE, BUT EVEN DURING
THOSE TIMES THE CITY WAS NOT IN TURMOIL AND THE PEOPLE OF
THE CITY NOT IN DANGER FROM THE SO-CALLED RIOTERS. OUTSIDE
THE HOURS OF THIS DESTRUCTIVE FURY, WHICH WAS SO NARROWLY
FOCUSED AND SO SPECIFICALLY LOCALIZED, THE CITY WAS QUIET,
AND PEOPLE WERE COMPLETELY SAFE EITHER ON OR OFF THE
STREETS.

2) KWANGJU WAS NOT A CITY HELD DANGEROUSLY BY STUDENTS OR
DISSIDENTS. IT WAS A CITY UNITED IN CRISIS. THE CRISIS
CAME FROM OUTSIDERS, UNITING THE CITIZENRY AS ONLY HAPPENS
IN CRISIS AND DISASTER. EVEN THE POLICE, EVEN THE RIOT-
POLICE, WERE FELT BY THE CITIZENS TO BE INNOCENT OF OFFENSE

AGAINST THE CITY. THE ANIMOSITY OF KWANGJU IS AGAINST THE
AIRBORNE UNIT WHICH BEHAVED SO BADLY, AND AGAINST THE CEN-
TRAL GOVERNMENT, WHICH THE CITY BELIEVES TO HAVE BEEN UN-
FAIR THROUGHOUT.

3) CIVIL RIGHTS, HUMAN RIGHTS, AND GREATER DEMOCRACY WERE
NOT AT THE HEART OF KWANGJU'S ANGER. STUDENT ACTIVITY TO-
WARD THESE GOALS WAS THE IMMEDIATE CAUSE OF THE EVENTS
WHICH ROUSED THE CITY, AND MANY OF THE CITIZENS FEEL DEEPLY

NNN

TEXT OF TELEGRAM 80SEOUL 007402

AUP265

PAGE 01   SEOUL 07402   10 OF 10   101223Z
ACTION EA-12

INFO OCT-01 ADS-00 CIAE-00 DODE-00 NSAE-00 NSCE-00
      SSO-00 ICAE-00 INRE-00 PM-05 H-01 INR-10 L-03
      PA-01 SP-02 SS-15 HA-05 IO-14 PC-01 OCS-06 SY-05
      SYE-00 DCT-02 /083 W
               ------------------015593   101344Z /43
O 100942Z JUN 80
FM AMEMBASSY SEOUL
TO SECSTATE WASHDC IMMEDIATE 6948
INFO AMEMBASSY TOKYO
COMUSKORFA SEOUL KS//BJ-IS
CHJUSMAG SEOUL KS
SA CINCUNC KS

C̶O̶N̶F̶I̶D̶E̶N̶T̶I̶A̶L SECTION 10 OF 10 SEOUL 07402

ABOUT THESE CAUSES, BUT THE KWANGJU INCIDENT WAS NOT FOR OR
BECAUSE OF THESE THINGS. IT WAS BECAUSE OF OUTRAGEOUS ACTS
AGAINST ITS PEOPLE, AND ITS OBJECTIVE WAS TO MAKE KNOWN
THAT SUCH ACTS COULD NOT BE INFLICTED HERE WITH IMPUNITY.

4) THE OUTRAGES WHICH OCCURRED WERE NOT FOR THEIR PART
DISCERNIBLY INFECTED WITH SEXUAL LICENSE OR WITH SADISTIC
ACTS AGAINST WOMEN. DESPITE RUMORS OF UNSPEAKABLE ACTS,
THE VICTIMS OF ABUSE PROVIDE INADEQUATE GROUNDS FOR BELIEF
IN SPECIFICALLY WOMAN-FOCUSED ATROCITIES.

5) TO THOSE WHO HAVE LIVED LONG IN KOREA, THE SINGLE MOST
AMAZING FACTOR IN THE ENTIRE KWANGJU INCIDENT IS AN ATYPI-
CAL AND PROBABLY MIRACULOUS RESTRAINT EXERCISED BY ALL.
WHATEVER CHARGES MAY BE BROUGHT AGAINST THE GOVERNMENT OR
THE MARTIAL LAW COMMAND, THE CONSPICUOUS FACT IS THAT,
WITHIN THE CONFINES OF THE KWANGJU AREA AND THE TIME OF
THE KWANGJU INCIDENT AFTER THE WITHDRAWAL OF THE AIRBORNE
UNITS, THE KOREAN MILITARY EXERCISED, AND THE KOREAN
GOVERNMENT ALLOWED, A RESTRAINT WHICH RAN COUNTER TO THEIR

RECORD AND MUST HAVE BEEN GALLING TO MAINTAIN. BY THE SAME
TOKEN, THE SELF-DISCIPLINE AND RESTRAINT SHOWN BY THE CITI-
ZENRY IS BEYOND ALLPRECEDENT.

FINALLY, THE MISSIONARIESWERE NOT IN ANY GREATDANGER, BUT
WERE THE OBJECT OF CONCERN ON THE PART NOT ONLY OF OUR OWN
COUNTRY BUT ALSO ONTHE PART OF KOREANSON BOTH SIDES OF
THE KWANGJU CONFLICT. NONETHELESS WELEARNED THAT HEROISM
IS APPARENTLY NOT REQUIRED OFGOD'SSERVANTS IN SITUATIONS

TEXT OF TELEGRAM BOSEOUL OO7402

LIKE OURS; BUT THAT HE GIVESINSTEAD A CLEAR CONSCIOUSNESS
OF WHAT WE SHOULDOR SHOULD NOT DO, TOGETHER WITH SO UN-
MISTAKABLE AN ASSURANCE OF HIS CARE THAT THERE IS NO ROOM
FOR THE KIND OF FEAR WHICH HEROISM CONQUERS. HAD THINGS
GONE DIFFERENTLY, OR SOME ACCIDENT OCCURRED, ONE OR MORE
OF US MIGHT HAVE DIED, BUT UNLESS IT IS HEROIC TO RELAX
IN THE LOVE OF GOD, WE NEVER FELT THAT HE WAS ASKING US TO
BE HIS HEROES.

THIS IS NOT TO SAY WE WERE IN SO CRITICAL A SITUATION, BUT
ONLY TO SAY WE WERE GIVEN STRONG AND SIMPLE GIFTS WHICH
MADE THESE THINGS IRRELEVANT.

/S/ [ ] JUNE 5-6, 1980. B/A9

END QUOTE. CLEYSTEEN

NNN

Annex 2. Gwangju Uprising Daily Log

May 14: The nation-wide university student union resolves to hold demonstrations off campus.

May 15: Tens of thousands of university students demonstrate in central Seoul.

May 16: Students in Seoul postpone further demonstrations. A peaceful torchlight rally is held by students in Gwangju.

May 17: University student leaders are detained during a meeting at Ewha Woman's University.

May 18: Martial law expands nation-wide. The National Assembly is suspended and universities are closed. Kim Young-sam is put under house arrest. Kim Dae-jung and Kim Jong-pil are detained. In Gwangju, the Seventh Special Warfare Brigade brutally suppresses protests by students and targets bystanders as well, angering citizens. The Gwangju Uprising begins.

May 19: Gwangju citizens join in the protest due to anger at the mounting casualties. The more citizens join, the more the military escalates its suppression of protesters. The first recorded deaths occur.

May 20: High schools in Gwangju are closed. Clashes increase in ferocity and people are beaten inhumanly. In the evening, dozens of taxis and city buses occupy downtown streets. Angered by distorted news broadcasts, citizens burn the MBC building. Night time clashes force the military to abandon almost all positions except Jeonnam Provincial Office.

May 21: Long distance phone lines are disconnected, cutting off Gwangju. Special warfare troops open fire on the thousands of protesters in front of the Jeonnam Provincial Office. Protesters take training weapons from a reservist armory. The uprising spreads to other towns in Jeonnam Province.

May 22: Protesters take over Jeonnam Provincial Office and Gwangju. The military stays outside of Gwangju and isolates the city from the rest of the country.

May 23: Protesters clean the streets of Gwangju. Special warfare troops open fire on mini-buses in Jeonnam village. Troops kill dozens on the outskirts of Gwangju.

May 24: Gwangju citizens continue to hold mass rallies and declare "Liberated Gwangju".

May 25: Markets and stores open, the city starts to recover.

May 26: The Citizens' Controlling Committee negotiates with the martial law officer, but the negotiations break down. Citizens warn of the possibility that the military may return at night. Women and children are sent home.

May 27: The military re-enters Gwangju. The citizen army promises to fight until the last minute and urges others to join them. Special warfare troops surround Jeonnam Provincial Office and storm it in the early morning, killing many citizen army members.

*This daily log has been reviewed by Choi Yong-ju and Matt VanVolkenburg.